Bildquellen:

sämtliche Illustrationen im Heft: © Boris Braun

S. 7: Königin Elizabeth II von England: © NASA/Bill Ingalls, Quelle: Wikimedia, gemeinfrei, da von der NASA zur Verfügung gestellt

S. 7: Karte: Commonwealth of Nations, © Applysense, Quelle: Wikimedia, gemeinfrei

S. 7: Hochzeit von Prince William und Catherine Middleton, © Robbie Dale, Quelle: Wikimedia, Creative Commons-Lizenz Namensnennung-Weitergabe unter gleichen Bedingungen 2.0 US-amerikanisch (nicht portiert)

S. 19: König Heinrich VIII (England), © Hans Holbein der Jüngere, Quelle: Wikimedia, gemeinfrei

S. 22: World Trade Center im März 2001, © Jeffmock, Quelle: Wikimedia, Creative Commons-Lizenz Namensnennung-Weitergabe unter gleichen Bedingungen 3.0 Unported

S. 22: Brennender Süddturm des World Trade Centers, © TheMachineStops, bearbeitet von upstateNYer, Quelle: Wikimedia, Creative Commons-Lizenz Namensnennung-Weitergabe unter gleichen Bedingungen 2.0 US-amerikanisch (nicht portiert)

S. 22: Opfer des 11. September 2001, © Don Halasy, Quelle: Wikimedia, gemeinfrei

S. 26: Untergehende Titanic: © Willy Stöwer (gezeichnet für das Magazin „Die Gartenlaube"), Quelle: Wikimedia, gemeinfrei

S. 29: Erdbeben- und Tsunamifolgen in Ofunato, Japan 1, © Matthew M. Bradley, Quelle: Wikimedia, gemeinfrei, da das Bild von einem Angehörigen der U.S. Navy aufgenommen wurde

S. 30: Erdbeben- und Tsunamifolgen in Ofunato, Japan 2, © Ethan Johnson, Quelle: Wikimedia, gemeinfrei, da das Bild von einem Angehörigen der U.S. Navy aufgenommen wurde

S. 30: Erdbeben- und Tsunamifolgen in Iwaki, Japan, © ryuki_a_g, Quelle: Wikimedia, Creative Commons-Lizenz Namensnennung 2.1 Japan

S. 34: trauriges Mädchen, © Jürgen Fälchle – Fotolia.com

S. 37: Aborigine, © francosperoni – Fotolia.com

S. 40: Karte der Besatzungszonen in Deutschland 1945, © glglgl, Quelle: Wikimedia, GNU Free Documentation License, Version 1.2 or any later version published by the Free Software Foundation; with no Invariant Sections, no Front-Cover Texts, and no Back-Cover Texts

S. 40: Menschen auf der Berliner Mauer, © Dr. Alexander Mayer, Quelle: Wikimedia, Creative Commons Attribution-Share Alike 3.0 Unported, 2.5 Generic, 2.0 Generic and 1.0 Generic license.

Für vollständigen Lizenztext „GNU Free Documentation License" siehe:
http://aol-verlag.de/gnu_free_documentation_license
Für vollständige Lizenztexte „Creative Commons-Lizenzvereinbarungen" siehe:
http://aol-verlag.de/creativecommons

Impressum

Englisch lesen und verstehen? No problem!

Anette Ruberg-Neuser (Jahrgang 1961) ist Grund-, Haupt- und Realschullehrerin und unterrichtet seit 1987 an einer Grund- und Verbundenen Haupt- und Realschule in Hessen. In den vergangenen Jahren hat sie umfangreiches Unterrichtsmaterial für Haupt- und Realschulklassen der Jahrgangsstufen 5–10 und für die an vielen hessischen Schulen angebotene Fördermaßnahme SchuB *(Schule und Betrieb)* erstellt und veröffentlicht.

1. Auflage 2013

Veritaskai 3 · 21079 Hamburg
Fon (040) 325083-060 · Fax (040) 325083-050
info@aol-verlag.de · www.aol-verlag.de

Redaktion: Kathrin Roth
Layout/Satz: Satzpunkt Ursula Ewert GmbH, Bayreuth
Coverfoto: © Mark Vickers – Fotolia.com

ISBN: 978-3-403-10148-2
Printed in Germany

Engagiert unterrichten. Natürlich lernen.

AOL verlag

Inhaltsverzeichnis

Vorwort

In den Bildungsstandards kommt der Lesekompetenz innerhalb der Sprachkompetenzen eine bedeutsame Stellung zu. Ohne angemessene Lesekompetenz ist ein erfolgreicher Lernprozess im Fremdsprachenunterricht schließlich auf Dauer nicht gewährleistet. Sie unterstützt und fördert entscheidend die Kommunikations- und Schreibkompetenz, denn das Lesen und Verstehen von Texten bietet sowohl Kommunikations- als auch Schreibanlässe.

Moderne Lehrwerke für den Englischunterricht bieten im Rahmen der einzelnen Units Texte, die zu deren jeweiligen Themenschwerpunkten passen. Meist „versteckt“ sich darin auch eine grammatische Besonderheit, z. B. eine neue Zeitform, Steigerungsformen, Adverbien – das Spektrum ist groß. Wir Lehrer sind dann oft geneigt, neben den inhaltlichen Aspekten eines Textes auch die grammatischen analysieren und so den Text zum Mittel zum Zweck werden zu lassen.
Ausnahmen sind in der Regel Texte, die sich meist im hinteren Bereich unserer Lehrbücher tummeln, oft unter der Überschrift „Extra Reading“. Je nach Lerngruppe sind sie mal mehr, mal weniger geeignet, abhängig von Inhalt, Länge und Wortschatz. Darüber hinaus bieten Lehrbuchtexte oft nur wenige verständnissichernde Übungsformate.
Dennoch planen viele Kollegen ihren Unterricht immer noch gerne streng nach den Vorgaben der Units. Ein mutiges Abweichen oder Weglassen von den dort vorgegebenen Texten und Übungsformaten zugunsten anderer, vor allem lehrbuchunabhängiger Inhalte, fällt vielen immer wieder schwer.

Doch warum nicht mal einen Text über das englische Königshaus, die Tsunamikatastrophe in Japan oder den Untergang der Titanic in den Unterricht einbauen und so bei den Schülern neues Interesse wecken?
Darüber hinaus ist sinnentnehmendes Lesen verschiedenartiger Texte ein wichtiger Aspekt in einer Welt, in der Englisch von immer größerer Bedeutung ist. Textverständnis wird heute in den meisten Bundesländern zum einen in landesspezifischen Lernstanderhebungen in verschiedenen Jahrgangsstufen, und zum anderen in den landesweiten schriftlichen Prüfungen zur Erlangung von Haupt- und Realschulabschlüssen überprüft.
Der frühzeitige Umgang mit Texten – losgelöst vom jeweiligen Lehrwerk – verbunden mit Übungsformaten, die auch in den Prüfungen vorkommen, ist daher von besonderer Bedeutung.

Neben verschiedenen und differenzierenden Übungsformaten zur Textverständnissicherung ist jedem Text in diesem Heft auch eine kleine Vokabelliste in Form von Fußnoten beigefügt. Nicht jedem Schüler wird diese Liste ausreichendes Textverständnis bieten. Deshalb halte ich es für wichtig, Schüler, die ihre Lesekompetenz schulen, frühzeitig im Umgang mit einem zweisprachigen Wörterbuch anzuleiten, sodass sie Vokabeln, die ihnen unbekannt sind oder die sie wieder vergessen haben, selbstständig und kompetent nachschlagen können.

Bei der Bearbeitung der Übungsformate zur Textverständnissicherung empfiehlt sich die Verwendung eines Lineals und Stifts oder Textmarkers zur Hervorhebung relevanter Textstellen, die z. B. bei der Beantwortung von Fragen zum Text, der Überprüfung von Right-Wrong-Aussagen oder bei der Suche von bestimmten Begriffen bedeutsam sind.

Unterstützt wird die Textarbeit durch eine durchgehende Zeilennummerierung, die sich auch bei der Besprechung der Aufgabenformate im Klassenplenum als vorteilhaft erweist.

Nur genaues Hinsehen, Vergleichen, Markieren und Sich-Einlassen auf die Texte können erfolgreiche Textarbeit gewährleisten und damit die Lesekompetenz nachhaltig und erfolgreich fördern.

Ich wünsche Ihnen, liebe Englischlehrer und -lehrerinnen, und Ihren Schülern viel Spaß beim Lesen.

Anette Ruberg-Neuser

Anette Ruberg-Neuser

Henry, the happy snowman

Christmas was over, and Sue and Ben Taylor were still waiting for snow. They wanted to try out the new sledges[1] their grandma had bought them for Christmas.

Then one night it snowed at last,[2] and in the morning streets, houses and trees were covered with wonderful white snow.

When Sue woke up and looked out of the window, she was very excited. 'Ben', she shouted. 'Wake up. There is snow everywhere. Quick, get up, and let's go outside.'

After breakfast they put on their anoraks, warm scarves, caps and Wellingtons[3], took their sledges and ran outside.

Ben's friend Tom and his little sister Mandy were outside, too. They started rolling big snowballs for a snowman.

'Hey', Ben shouted. 'We want to try[4] our new sledges. Are you coming?'

'Sure,' Tom answered. 'But first we want to finish this snowman. You can help us.'

Ben helped Tom with two big snowballs. They put the snowballs on top of one another. Sue and Mandy rolled a smaller snowball that they put on top of the big snowball. That was the head.

'We must make him a nice face', Sue said. 'Yes,' Mandy said, 'and we must put a real hat on his head, too.'

Tom ran into the house and fetched a carrot for the nose and some nuts for the mouth. Two stones from the garden were the eyes. Sue found her father's old hat in the garage, and Mandy fetched one of her scarves and put it around the snowman's neck. Now the snowman looked really nice, and the children were happy.

Suddenly the snowman began to talk. 'Hello, thank you for making me. I'm a very nice snowman. By the way, my name is Henry. I'd like to be your friend.'

Then the snowman began to jump up and down in the garden.

First the children were shocked, and Mandy nearly started to cry because she was a bit frightened[5]. But then they all jumped with Henry up and down in the garden.

The children fetched their sledges and went down the hill at the end of their street. Henry also slid[6] down the hill, and they all had a great time.

In the evening, Henry stayed in the garden. On the following days Sue, Ben, Mandy, and Tom played with him or took him to the hill at the end of their street where the children went down on their sledges.

There were a lot of children now because they all wanted to see Henry. He took some of the smaller children on his back and slid down the hill with them. Then Henry jumped up and down and shouted, 'Oh, I'm so happy. Let's slide again.' Then he jumped up the hill and slid downhill again with more children on his back.

Then one afternoon it started to snow again. Suddenly the snowfall was so heavy[7] that the children had problems seeing where the sledges were taking them.

'Let's go home', Sue said to Ben and Henry. But they enjoyed the snow so much that they didn't want to go home.

'I want to slide downhill one more time', Henry said. And Ben said, 'Yes, and I want to go downhill one more time, too.'

Henry slid downhill and soon Sue and Ben could not see him anymore. Then Ben sat on his sledge and started his trip downhill. He couldn't see where he was going. Suddenly he crashed into some deep snow and fell off his sledge. Somebody cried out, 'Ouch, my belly[8]'. When Ben stood up and looked for his sledge he saw Henry. Henry was on his back, and there was a big hole[9] in his belly. 'You crashed into me, Ben', he said, 'and now there is a big hole in my belly.' 'Oh no', Ben cried. 'I'm so sorry, Henry.' He called for Sue, Tom, and Mandy. When they arrived they carefully lifted Henry on one of the sledges. They pulled him uphill, and it took them a long time because Henry was so heavy.

Back in the Taylor's garden the children filled the hole in Henry's belly with snow. When Henry looked like a real snowman again he said, 'Thank you, children. Now I need a rest.' The children left Henry in the garden, but the following day he was gone.

The children looked for him everywhere, behind the trees and in the street, but Henry was not there. They were very sad and Ben cried. He said, 'It is my fault[10]. I hurt him and now he left us.' Ben was so unhappy that he didn't want to eat his breakfast, and he didn't want to play with the others.

When Mrs Taylor opened the postbox later that morning she found a note. It was from Henry.

First the children were a little sad. But then they understood that Henry wanted to make some more children happy that winter. And Ben was happy that Henry was still his friend.

Hello children,

My belly is okay again. It wasn't Ben's fault that he crashed into me. The snowfall was so heavy. Thank you for a wonderful time. But now I must leave. I must visit some more children before the end of winter.

Next year I will see you again.

Love, Henry

1) sledge – Schlitten
2) at last – endlich
3) Wellingtons – Gummistiefel
4) to try – ausprobieren, testen
5) to be frightened – ängstlich sein
6) to slide / slid – rutschen
7) heavy – hier: stark, heftig
8) belly – Bauch
9) hole – Loch
10) fault – Schuld, Fehler

Let's check

In den folgenden Übungen kannst du zeigen, wie gut du den Text verstanden hast. Während der Bearbeitung der einzelnen Aufgaben solltest du deine Lösungen immer mit dem Text vergleichen.

1. Matching sentences

Match the parts of the sentences correctly, then match the numbers with the letters in the small list below.

1	When it began to snow, Ben and Sue	a	he could slide downhill with all the children.
2	But first they helped their friends	b	crashed into Henry.
3	When the snowman was ready,	c	Henry was gone.
4	His name was Henry and	d	Henry was very tired.
5	They all had a great time when	e	he wanted to visit other children, too.
6	Henry was always very happy when	f	it was his fault.
7	One afternoon there	g	in Henry's belly.
8	Henry and Ben	h	Tom and Mandy to build a snowman.
9	But then Ben	i	wanted to slide down the hill one more time.
10	There was a big hole	j	they slid down the hill at the end of their street.
11	After they had filled the hole with snow,	k	a note from Henry in the postbox.
12	The next morning	l	he began to talk and to jump.
13	Ben thought that	m	wanted to try their new sledges.
14	Then Mrs Taylor found	n	he wanted to be the children's friend.
15	Henry had left because	o	was heavy snowfall.

1	2	3	4	5	6	7	8	9	10	11	12	13	14	15

Now write the sentences into your exercise book. You will get a summary of the text.

2. Questions on the text

Lies jede Frage zunächst genau und überlege, wonach gefragt wird. Finde im Text die Textstelle, die dir die Antwort auf die Frage gibt, und unterstreiche sie. Schreibe vollständige Antworten im Simple Past.

a) What did Sue and Ben get from their grandma for Christmas?

They got new sledges from their grandma.

b) What did the children fetch for the snowman's face?

c) What did the snowman suddenly do?

d) Why did Mandy nearly start to cry?

e) Why didn't Ben and Henry want to go home when the heavy snowfall started?

f) Why did Ben crash into Henry?

g) What was wrong with Henry?

h) Why were the children sad the following morning?

i) What did Mrs Taylor find in the postbox?

j) Who did Henry want to visit before the end of winter?

3. What is wrong in the following sentences?

Vergleiche die folgenden Sätze mit dem Text. Manchmal ist mehr als ein Wort falsch.

a) When Sue looked out of the window and saw the snow, she was very ~~sad~~. excited
b) After lunch the children put on their anoraks, scarves, hats and Wellingtons. ____________
c) Tom fetched a cucumber for the nose and stones for the mouth. ____________
d) The snowman jumped up and down in the street. ____________
e) The children fetched their skateboards and went down the hill. ____________
f) Henry put the bigger children on his belly and slid downhill with them. ____________
g) One afternoon it started to rain again. ____________
h) 'You crashed into me, Tom, and now there is a big hole in my head.' ____________
i) Mrs Taylor filled the hole in Henry's back with stones. ____________
j) Henry left the children because he wanted to visit his parents. ____________

4. Put the pictures and the sentences in the right order.

Schneide die Bilder und die Sätze aus und klebe sie in der richtigen Reihenfolge in dein Heft.

a) Then Ben crashed into Henry in the heavy snowfall.	e) The following morning Henry was gone.
b) Henry and the children enjoyed sliding down a hill.	f) After Christmas Ben, Sue and their friends made a snowman.
c) The children filled the hole in Henry's belly with snow again.	g) Suddenly, Henry the snowman began to talk and jump.
d) In a note Henry wrote that he wanted to visit other children, too.	h) Henry took the smaller children on his back.

The Royals[1]

This is Queen Elizabeth II. She was born on 21st April, 1926. She became queen after her father George VI died in 1952. In 2012 she celebrated 60 years on the throne. Only Queen Victoria, the Queen's great-great-grandmother, ruled[2] Britain for longer (almost 64 years). The Queen is married to Prince Philip, the Duke[3] of Edinburgh, who turned 90 in 2011.

Elizabeth is not only the Queen of Great Britain but also of the 54 so-called Commonwealth countries. These are the states that in former[4] times were British colonies. So the Queen is still the sovereign[5] of Canada and Australia for example.

Queen Elizabeth II. and Prince Philip have four children: Prince Charles, Princess Anne, Prince Andrew, and Prince Edward.
Prince Charles, the Prince of Wales, was born in Buckingham Palace in 1948. After school he studied at Cambridge University. Later he became a helicopter pilot, then he went to the navy[6] and was captain of a ship.
In 1981 he married Lady Diana Spencer. They had two sons, William (born 1982) and Harry (born 1984). Lady Diana was very popular and people called her their Queen of Hearts. But the marriage[7] was not very happy. Charles and Diana got a divorce[8] in August 1996. Diana was killed in a car accident while in Paris on 31st August, 1997. In 2005 Charles married Camilla Parker-Bowles. She was Prince Charles's former girlfriend and the love of his life.

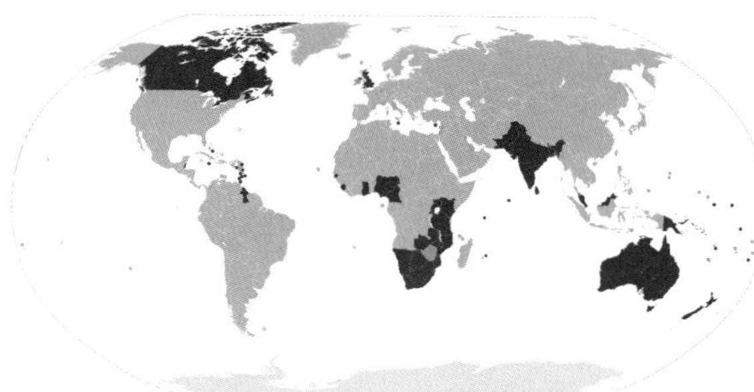

On 29 April, 2011 Prince Charles's eldest son, Prince William, married Kate Middleton. They had been friends for a long time. This was a holiday in the UK, so most people didn't go to work, and pupils didn't go to school. The wedding[9] took place in Westminster Abbey, the church of the kings and queens in London. Thousands of people watched Kate and William in their carriage[10] in the streets of London, and millions of people all over the world watched the wedding on TV.

The majority[11] of the British people are proud[12] to have one of the oldest monarchies in the world, and most love their Queen. She is the 66th monarch of England and Great Britain over a period of 1500 years. And, of course, they love Prince William, who will be the future king of Great Britain, perhaps even after Queen Elizabeth, if his father Charles abstains[13] from the throne.
Since their wedding Kate and William have lived in an old farm house in North Wales. Prince William works there as a helicopter pilot in the British military. Kate is expecting her first baby in the summer of 2013.

National Anthem[14]

God save our gracious[15] Queen,
Long live our noble Queen,
God save the Queen!
Send her victorious[16],
Happy and glorious,
Long to reign over us;
God save the Queen!

1) the Royals – die königliche Familie
2) to rule – herrschen, regieren
3) duke – Herzog
4) former – frühere/r
5) sovereign – Herrscher/in
6) navy – Marine
7) marriage – Ehe
8) to get a divorce – sich scheiden lassen
9) wedding – Hochzeit, Trauung
10) carriage – Kutsche
11) majority – Mehrheit
12) to be proud – stolz sein
13) to abstain from – auf etwas verzichten
14) national anthem – Nationalhymne
15) gracious – gütig, gnädig
16) victorious – siegreich

Let's check

In den folgenden Übungen kannst du zeigen, wie gut du den Text verstanden hast. Während der Bearbeitung der einzelnen Aufgaben solltest du deine Lösungen immer mit dem Text vergleichen.

1. Matching sentences

Match the parts of the sentences correctly, then match the numbers with the letters in the small list below.

1	In 2012 Queen Elizabeth II.	a	eldest son.
2	Her husband is	b	Kate and William moved to North Wales.
3	Elizabeth is also Queen of	c	as a helicopter pilot.
4	Prince Charles is the Queen's	d	Lady Diana Spencer.
5	He was first married to	e	in a terrible car crash in Paris.
6	She died	f	married Kate Middleton.
7	In 2005 Prince Charles	g	celebrated 60 years on the throne.
8	On 29 April, 2011 Prince William	h	married Camilla, the love of his life.
9	After the wedding	i	Australia and Canada.
10	Prince William works	j	the Duke of Edinburgh.

1	2	3	4	5	6	7	8	9	10

2. Have you checked your sentences? Then write them down. You'll get a summary of the text.

____

____

____

____

____

____

____

3. Fill in the grid. Can you find the correct answer?

She is married to Prince William.

He is five years older than the Queen.

He is the youngest child of the Queen.

He was the Queen's father.

She was Queen for almost 64 years.

She was the Queen of Hearts.

She is Charles's sister.

Prince Charles is married to her.

He can be the next king.

The answer is ____________ ______________________________.

4. Let's check in German.

Welcher Satz im Text sagt aus, dass ...

a) die Queen auch Königin über andere Länder ist.

line: ______ Sentence: ____

b) Prince Charles an einer Universität studiert hat.

line: ______ Sentence: ____

c) Lady Diana sehr beliebt war.

line: ______ Sentence: ____

d) der Hochzeitstag von Kate Middleton und Prince William ein besonderer (Feier)tag war.

line: ______ Sentence: ____

e) sie sich bereits lange kannten, bevor sie heirateten.

line: ______ Sentence: ____

f) die meisten Briten ihre Königin lieben.

line: ______ Sentence: ____

5. Find the correct expression in the text for ...

a) a king or a queen: ____________________

b) states that were British colonies once: ____________________

c) a horse-drawn vehicle: ____________________

d) someone who flies a helicopter: ____________________

e) more than half: ____________________

f) the ceremony in which two people come together as wife and husband: ____________________

A visit at Buckingham Palace

The pupils of class 6E of *Fulston Manor School* in Sittingbourne, Kent, did a history project. Every pupil chose a king or queen of England and tried to find out as much as possible about that monarch.

Pete was interested in William the Conqueror who was the first Norman[1] King of England. Melinda wanted to find out all about Henry VIII and his six wives, and Brenda read all about Queen Victoria who reigned from 1837 to 1901.

Steve couldn't decide[2] at first, but then he chose Queen Elizabeth II. He found a lot of facts and photos of his Queen on the Internet and in books he borrowed[3] from the school library. One Saturday, when he was reading about the Queen's coronation,[4] he had an idea. All his classmates did a project on kings and queens who had died[5] a long time ago, but his Queen was still alive! Why not ask her for a meeting?

That same evening he wrote a letter to Buckingham Palace:

> Her Majesty Queen Elizabeth II.
> Buckingham Palace
> London SW1A 1AA
>
> Madam,
> Our class at Fulston Manor School in Sittingbourne are doing a history project on the kings and queens of England.
> I chose Your Majesty[6]. I have already read a lot about Your Majesty's reign.[7]
> Please allow me to ask if it would be possible to visit Your Majesty in Buckingham Palace?
> It would be so wonderful to see and talk to a real queen.
>
> I have the honour to be, Madam, Your Majesty's humble and obedient servant[8].
> Steve Wilson

Steve mailed his letter the following morning before he went to school. About a week later, when he came home from school, he found a letter with a Royal coat of arms[9] on the kitchen table. His hands were shaking when he opened it. He couldn't believe it. Steve and all the pupils of his class were invited to meet the Queen at Buckingham Palace.

Three weeks later, when the boys and girls of class 6E got off the train at Victoria Station, they were all very excited. It was only a five-minute walk to Buckingham Palace. They entered it by a side entrance[10]. A servant[11] showed them some of the state rooms[12] usually open to visitors when the Queen is on holiday in Scotland. They loved the big and richly decorated rooms.

Then they were shown into a big room with a large table in the middle. The servant said, 'Sit down, please. Her Majesty will soon be here to see you.' A few minutes later the door opened, and the servant said, 'Her Majesty, Queen Elizabeth II. Please rise[13].'

The pupils and their teacher rose, and the Queen entered the room. 'Be seated', she said. Everybody sat down and the Queen went on, 'I am pleased to welcome you at Buckingham Palace today. I understand that you are doing a history project on the kings and queens of our country. I therefore have a little present for you.'

The servant put a box on a side table and the Queen went on, 'Here is a poster for every pupil with the names of all our kings and queens in a chronological order. I signed[14] it personally. Will you now come forward one by one and receive your present, please, but I would like Steve Wilson to be the first.'

Steve was very excited when he went up to the Queen. She offered him her right hand, and Steve shook it and bowed[15]. 'Welcome Steve', the Queen said. 'I usually do not read so many letters personally, but my secretary showed me yours and I was very pleased. Here is your poster, Steve, and I have got another special present for you.' The servant passed the Queen a small box, and she gave it to Steve. It was a special tea cup with a picture of the Queen painted on it. 'Thank you, Ma'am', Steve said, bowed and quickly went back to his seat at the table.

Then all the other boys and girls got their posters, and the Queen said good-bye and left. The servant gave the pupils some biscuits and soft drinks and then they left Buckingham Palace and went home by train. Steve put his tea cup on the shelf above his bed where he could look at it every night before he went to sleep.

1) Norman – normannisch (aus der Normandie in Nordfrankreich stammend)
2) to decide – (sich) entscheiden
3) to borrow – ausleihen
4) coronation – Krönung
5) to die – sterben
6) Your Majesty – Ihre Majestät (förmliche Anrede der Königin)
7) reign – Regierungszeit
8) I have the honour to be Your Majesty's humble and obedient servant – Es ist mir eine Ehre, ein demütiger und ergebener Diener Ihrer Majestät zu sein *(Grußformel am Ende eines Briefes an die englische Königin)*
9) Royal coat of arms – königliches Wappen
10) side entrance – Seiteneingang
11) servant – Bediensteter
12) state rooms – prunkvolle Staatsräume im Buckingham Palast
13) to rise / rose – sich erheben
14) to sign – unterschreiben
15) to bow – sich verneigen

Let's check

In den folgenden Übungen kannst du zeigen, wie gut du den Text verstanden hast. Während der Bearbeitung der einzelnen Aufgaben solltest du deine Lösungen immer mit dem Text vergleichen.

1. Which ending fits best?

Compare with the text. There is only one correct ending for each sentence.

1. Steve's class at Fulston Manor school
   - ☐ a) did a project on Queen Elizabeth II.
   - ☐ b) did a history project on the English monarchs.
   - ☐ c) had to find out as much as possible about the kings and queens of England.
2. Steve Wilson
   - ☐ a) was interested in Queen Mary I.
   - ☐ b) didn't want to choose Queen Elizabeth II.
   - ☐ c) wanted to do his project on Queen Elizabeth II.
3. So he tried to find out more about her
   - ☐ a) on the Internet.
   - ☐ b) at the library in Sittingbourne.
   - ☐ c) on TV.
4. After that Steve
   - ☐ a) went to London to have a look at Buckingham Palace.
   - ☐ b) wrote a letter to the Queen.
   - ☐ c) read a book about the Queen's coronation.
5. A few days later
   - ☐ a) Steve mailed his letter to the Queen.
   - ☐ b) he found a postcard from London on the kitchen table.
   - ☐ c) he and his class got an invitation to Buckingham Palace.
6. At Buckingham Palace
   - ☐ a) they were shown the richly decorated state rooms.
   - ☐ b) the servants were very unfriendly to the pupils.
   - ☐ c) they had to wait for the Queen for more than an hour.
7. Then the Queen
   - ☐ a) showed class 6E into a big room with a large table.
   - ☐ b) welcomed the boys and girls of class 6E.
   - ☐ c) asked class 6E to rise.
8. She gave each of them
   - ☐ a) a box with a present in it.
   - ☐ b) a special tea cup.
   - ☐ c) a signed poster with the names of the English kings and queens.
9. She also had
   - ☐ a) biscuits and a soft drink for the pupils.
   - ☐ b) a letter for Steve.
   - ☐ c) a tea cup as a special present for Steve.

2. A summary of the text

Write the correct sentences in your exercise book. You will get a short summary of the text.

Start like this:
Steve's class at Fulston Manor School did a history project on the English monarchs.

3. Find the right order of the following sentences.

At Buckingham Palace:

- [ ] *'Here is a poster for every pupil.'*
- [ ] *'I would like Steve Wilson to be the first.'*
- [ ] *'Be seated.'*
- [ ] *'I am pleased to welcome you at Buckingham Palace today.'*
- [1] *'Her Majesty will soon be here to see you.'*
- [ ] *'Thank you, Ma'am.'*
- [ ] *'Please rise.'*
- [ ] *'I have got a special present for you.'*
- [ ] *'I usually do not read so many letters personally.'*

4. Can you get it right?

In die folgenden Sätze haben sich kleine Fehler eingeschlichen. Findest du sie? Unterstreiche die Fehler und schreibe die richtigen Begriffe auf die Zeilen rechts neben den Sätzen!

a) The pupils of Fulston Manor School in Salisbury did a history project. ____________________

b) Steve wanted to ask the Queen for a book about her coronation. ____________________

c) One day he found a letter with a crown on the kitchen table. ____________________

d) The walk from Victoria Station to Buckingham Palace only took ten minutes. ____________________

e) Visitors can see the state rooms when the Queen is working in Scotland. ____________________

f) The pupils and the teacher sat down when the Queen came in. ____________________

g) The names of the kings and queens on the poster were in alphabetical order. ____________________

h) Steve was very nervous when he went up to the Queen. ____________________

i) Steve shook the Queen's hand and said hello to her. ____________________

j) The Queen gave Steve a box with her picture on it. ____________________

5. Find the correct expression in the text for ...

a) taking and using something that belongs to somebody else and returning it later:

____

b) a title of respect when speaking to a king or queen: ____________________

c) going into a building: ____________________

d) moving downwards to greet a person of respect: ____________________

e) someone working or writing letters for another person: ____________________

The bike trip

David and Nick decided to go on a bike trip on their new mountain bikes. They wanted to have a picnic somewhere in the forest. David's mother prepared some sandwiches, and Nick's mother bought two big bottles of lemonade each.

At 9 am on a Saturday morning David picked up Nick at his house. Mrs Carins, Nick's mother, asked her son, 'Did you put your mobile phone into your saddlebag, Nick?'

'Sure, mum', Nick answered.

'Well, if anything goes wrong, please call me at once', Mrs Carins said.

'Don't worry, mum, everything will be fine.'

Then the two boys were on their way. After five miles along a busy[1] road they turned into a side street. Here they felt safer because there weren't so many cars. They cycled along this road for another 4 miles. Then they turned into a forest path[2] that led to a lake. The boys decided to go to the lake first, perhaps swim in it, and then have their picnic. After three miles on the forest path, David and Nick stopped. It was hot, and so they drank some of their lemonade. When they were getting on their bikes again, Nick suddenly winced.[3]

'Ouch,' he said and held the right side of his stomach.

'What's wrong?', David asked.

'I am not sure. But my right side is suddenly hurting.'

'I am sure it's that lemonade. Perhaps you only drank too much too quickly.' – 'You are probably[4] right. Let's go. The pain[5] will soon be over.'

But they didn't get far. Nick had to stop again. He sat down and leaned against a tree.

'I think I can't go on. It's hurting so much.'

'Alright, do you think you can ride your bike back home?', David asked.

'I don't think so. I can't even get up', Nick said and began to cry.

'Don't worry, Nick. Give me your mobile, and I will call your mum. She can pick you up and take you to the doctor's.'

David found Nick's mobile phone in the saddlebag. It was on, and David dialled Mrs Carins's number. Suddenly he heard a beep,[6] and on the display the words LOW BATTERY appeared[7] in big red letters. At the other end of the line Mrs Carins answered the phone. But before David could say anything the mobile went dead.

'Oh darn! Your mobile is dead'. David shouted.

'Oh no', Nick said. 'I left it on for three days, and I forgot to recharge[8] it. Oh David, now we can't call my mum.'

'I'll go and get help', David said. 'I'll ride to the lake. It isn't far now. I'll find someone with a mobile to call your mum.'

When David walked to his bike Nick cried, 'David, please don't leave me. I think I've got appendicitis[9]. It hurts so much.'

David was very excited now. 'But I've got to get help', he said.

'No, please stay here. Perhaps somebody with a mobile will come along this path soon.'

They waited for almost two hours, but nobody came. Nick's stomach was hurting badly.

Suddenly they heard a car. It came slowly towards the boys. It was Mrs Carins. When she saw the boys, she stopped and got out.

'Mum', Nick shouted, 'how did you find us?'

'When I got your call and your mobile went dead, I suddenly thought that something was wrong. So I tried to find you. I know how much you two love lakes. Now, what's wrong, darling?'

Nick told his mother, and quickly she took him to the hospital where he had an operation the same day.

1) busy – belebt
2) forest path – Waldweg
3) to wince – zucken
4) probably – wahrscheinlich
5) pain – Schmerz
6) beep – Piepton
7) to appear – erscheinen
8) to recharge – wieder aufladen
9) appendicitis – Blinddarmentzündung

Let's check

In den folgenden Übungen kannst du zeigen, wie gut du den Text verstanden hast. Während der Bearbeitung der einzelnen Aufgaben solltest du deine Lösungen immer mit dem Text vergleichen.

1. Right or wrong?

	right	wrong
a) Nick and David wanted to go to the mountains on their bikes.		
b) Nick's mother bought something to drink for the boys.		
c) Nick put his mobile phone into his saddlebag.		
d) The boys cycled four miles and then they turned into a forest path.		
e) After Nick had drunk some lemonade, his stomach began to hurt.		
f) When the pain didn't stop, the boys cycled back.		
g) The battery of Nick's mobile was low.		
h) David told Mrs Carins about Nick's problems.		
i) Nick recharged his mobile two days ago.		
j) David rode to the lake to get some help.		
k) Nick didn't want David to leave him to find help.		
l) After more than two hours, Mrs Carins found the boys.		
m) Nick had an operation the same day.		

2. Please correct the sentences that are wrong in No. 1. *(There are six.)*

____

____

____

____

____

____

3. Find an expression in the text for …

a) a telephone that you can take with you: ______________________________

b) a part of the body: ______________________________

c) something in a mobile that you must recharge: ______________________________

d) a meal you take and eat outdoors: ______________________________

e) a big plant that grows in a forest: ______________________________

f) a building where you take sick people: ______________________________

g) riding a bike: ______________________________

h) the opposite of near: ______________________________

4. Finish the sentences.

Ergänze die folgenden Satzanfänge mithilfe des Textes.

a) One Saturday morning David and Nick ______________________________

b) Nick put his mobile phone ______________________________

c) The boys wanted to go ______________________________

d) After a few miles on the forest path, they stopped and ______________________________

e) Suddenly Nick winced and held ______________________________

f) Then Nick sat down and ______________________________

g) Nick's stomach hurt so much that he started ______________________________

h) David called Nick's mother but before he could tell her anything ______________________________

____

i) Nick had forgotten to ______________________________

j) David wanted to ride to the lake to ______________________________

k) But Nick said, 'David, please ______________________________

l) The boys waited ______________________________

m) Then Mrs Carins arrived in her car and took ______________________________

____

5. Find the correct order of the text.

Schneide die Textstreifen aus und klebe sie in der richtigen Reihenfolge in dein Heft!

The battery of Nick's mobile was low.
David wanted to find help at the lake.
Nick and David went on a bike trip on a Saturday morning.
He couldn't go on because the pain was getting worse.
But Nick didn't want to stay alone.
Their mothers gave them something to eat and drink for a picnic.
After nine miles on the roads, the boys turned into a forest path.
They drank some of their lemonade because it was hot.
Quickly she took her son to hospital.
Mrs Carins found the boys after more than two hours.
Suddenly Nick felt a terrible pain in his stomach.
They wanted to go to a lake and have a picnic.
When Mrs Carins answered the phone, Nick's mobile went dead.
Nick put his mobile phone into his saddlebag.

A photo of the monster

In their summer holidays Martin, Sam, and David from Aberdeen in Scotland went to Inverness by bike. They wanted to see the famous Loch Ness. Many people think that there is a monster called Nessie in the lake.

It took them three days on their bikes. In the afternoon of the third day they arrived in Inverness. Then they found a room at the youth hostel[1].

The following morning Martin woke up at seven o'clock and went to the window. 'It's raining', he said to Sam and David who were still lying in bed. 'I think we can't go on a bike tour today.'

'Don't worry, Martin', Sam said. 'We can have a quiet day at the lake and visit Nessie. There won't be so many tourists today if the weather is getting worse.'

After breakfast the boys left the youth hostel and walked to the lake. There were some adverts[2] and a price list for boat rentals[3].

'We could go for a boat trip on the lake', David said. 'Too expensive', Sam answered. 'My parents didn't give me so much money.'

Then it started to rain.

'I won't stand here in the rain and get wet', Sam said. 'There's a little café over there. Let's have a drink and wait for the sun.'

The boys went towards[4] the café. They passed a souvenir shop. There were lots of little plastic models of Nessie in the shop window.

'Great', Martin said. 'I'd like to have a look inside. Are you coming?'

'Sure', David said, but Sam didn't want to go inside. 'I'm not spending any money on silly plastic monsters', he said. 'I'll go over to the café and wait for you.'

Sam left his friends and went to the café, and Martin and David went into the souvenir shop. They bought two big plastic models of the monster. They were £ 4.80 each.

When they came out of the shop, it was raining harder. Some tourists were standing near the lake and watching the water. Suddenly a man shouted, 'Look, the monster!' He pointed to something black in the water. Everybody looked ... but it was only a piece of wood[5].

'They are all waiting for Nessie', David said. 'I'm sure she doesn't like the rain.'

'Of course she does', Martin answered. 'Take a photo of her!'

'Very funny, Martin', David said. 'I can't take a photo of Nessie if she isn't here.'

Martin opened his rucksack and took out his plastic model. 'Here she is. Take out your digital camera, and I'll put Nessie in the water.' David started to laugh. 'What a great idea. We'll show the photo to Sam.'

Martin wanted to put the model into the water, but he slipped, and his feet got wet[6]. 'Blimey', he shouted. 'I hate wet feet!' He put the model on the waves[7]. David took the photo. Then they went to the café to meet Sam.

'Hi Sam, look what we've got', Martin shouted and showed Sam the photo on the display of his digital camera.

'What's that? Did you really see the monster? Why didn't you tell me?'

Sam was very excited. The other people at the café turned their heads and looked at the boys.

'Calm down, Sam', Martin said. 'And let's go back to the youth hostel because I can't stand[8] wet feet.'

1) youth hostel – Jugendherberge
2) advert – Reklame
3) boat rental – Mietboot
4) towards – in Richtung
5) piece of wood – Holzstück
6) wet – nass
7) wave – Welle
8) to stand sth. – etwas ertragen, ausstehen

Let's check

In den folgenden Übungen kannst du zeigen, wie gut du den Text verstanden hast. Während der Bearbeitung der einzelnen Aufgaben solltest du deine Lösungen immer mit dem Text vergleichen.

1. Right or wrong?

	right	wrong
a) Martin, David, and Sam arrived in Inverness by bus.		
b) On their first day in Inverness the boys were too tired to go on a bike tour.		
c) They went to the lake because the weather wasn't nice.		
d) Sam didn't want to go on a boat trip because it was too expensive.		
e) When it started to rain, the boys went to a fast food restaurant.		
f) David and Martin bought plastic models of Nessie.		
g) There weren't a lot of tourists at the lake.		
h) One of the tourists saw Nessie.		
i) Martin put his plastic model into the water and David took a photo of it.		
j) Martin fell into the lake and was completely wet.		
k) Sam believed[1] that his friends had seen the monster.		
l) The other people in the café also wanted to see the photo of the monster.		

2. Please correct the sentences that are wrong in No. 1. *(There are six.)*

____

____

____

____

____

____

3. Find an expression in the text for …

a) someone who visits interesting places: ______________________________

b) costing a lot of money: ______________________________

c) a place where you can have a hot drink: ______________________________

d) speaking in a loud voice: ______________________________

e) the two parts of the body that you walk on: ______________________________

f) the opposite of dry: ______________________________

4. Write your own story.

When Martin came home, he told his parents the story of the photo.

a) On our first day in Inverness the weather ______________________________

b) So we went ______________________________

c) We didn't rent a boat because ______________________________

d) Then Sam went ______________________________

e) David and I bought ______________________________

f) We went back ______________________________

g) Then a man shouted, ____________________ but it was only ____________________

____

h) Then I put ______________________________ and
David took ______________________________

i) We showed ______________________________

j) Sam was very ______________ and ______________________________

1) to believe – glauben

5. Questions – answers – pictures.

On this page you find questions and answers on the text. There are more answers than you need. Cut out the questions and answers, put them in the right order and stick them correctly in your exercise book. Then cut out the pictures and stick them next to the correct questions and answers.

⑤ **What did David and Martin show to Sam in the café?**	② **Why did David take out his digital camera?**
⑦ **What did one of the tourists suddenly think?**	① **Why did David and Martin go into a souvenir shop?**
⑥ **Why did Sam go to a café?**	⑧ **Why didn't the boys go on a boat trip on Loch Ness?**
④ **What was the weather like on their first day in Inverness?**	③ **Where did Martin and his friends go in their summer holidays?**
Ⓓ *Because they wanted to buy plastic models of Nessie.*	Ⓕ *Because Martin's feet got wet.*
Ⓚ *Because he didn't want to spend money on a plastic model of Nessie.*	Ⓑ *It was very expensive and Sam didn't have enough money.*
Ⓔ *They went from Aberdeen to Inverness by bike.*	Ⓗ *He thought he saw Nessie, but it was only a piece of wood.*
Ⓒ *They showed him their photo of Nessie.*	Ⓐ *It was raining.*
Ⓘ *Because he wanted to take a photo of Martin's Nessie model in the water.*	Ⓖ *The models cost £ 4.80 each.*

King Henry VIII

The people of England have always been very proud of their kings and queens. The British monarchy has a very long tradition. Queen Elizabeth II is the 40th monarch since William the Conqueror crossed the Channel from France in 1066. He invaded England and became the first Norman[1)] king.

But none of Britain's kings has been as unique[2)] as king number 20, King Henry VIII. Henry was only 18 when he became king in 1509. He loved dancing and hunting but even more than that he loved eating and drinking. He became famous because of his six wives. Of course he didn't have them all at the same time, but one after the other. How did it happen? Well, his first wife was the Spanish Princess Catherine of Aragon. She was the widow of his elder brother Arthur. For an English monarch at that time it was very important to have a son who would be the heir[3)] to the throne. But Catherine didn't have a son. She gave birth to a daughter, Mary. Henry was very disappointed and wanted a divorce. He asked the pope in Rome to grant him a divorce from Catherine, but the pope refused[4)].

In 1533 he married Anne Boleyn although Catherine was officially still his wife. The pope excommunicated[5)] him, and Henry broke with Rome. He made himself head of the new Church of England. Now he could divorce Catherine. As long as she lived she never accepted the divorce and always hoped that Henry would come back to her. In the meantime Henry grew tired of Anne Boleyn, who couldn't produce a male heir. She had a daughter, Elizabeth. In 1536 Henry started courting[6)] Jane Seymour. He had to get rid[7)] of Anne and accused[8)] her of a love affair with her own brother. She was sent to the Tower of London and executed in 1536. Only a few days later Henry married Jane Seymour, his third wife and love of his life. She fulfilled Henry's greatest wish and gave birth to his son, Edward. But then Jane died only days after childbirth. Henry was so sad that he didn't want to have another wife. He took care of his son who was often ill. It would have been terrible for Henry if he had lost Edward, too. Edward wasn't Henry's only son. Outside his marriages Henry had affairs with a number of mistresses[9)]. One of them gave birth to his son Henry Fitzroy. But as an illegitimate son he could not become king of England.

Henry's Lord Chancellor[10)] advised Henry to marry the German princess Anne of Cleves. Henry agreed without knowing what she looked like. When she arrived in England in 1540, he was shocked, because Anne was ugly and Henry didn't like her. Nonetheless,[11)] Henry married her for political reasons. The marriage was annulled[12)] only six months later. It is said that Anne didn't allow Henry to touch her, and so he could not have another son with her. Out of respect that Anne didn't protest against the annulment he let her live in one of his palaces and often invited her to court[13)].

Wife number five was Catherine Howard. She was nearly 30 years younger than Henry when he married her in July 1540. At that time Henry weighed about 140 kilograms and had an open leg wound. Perhaps that was one of the reasons why Catherine started an affair with one of Henry's servants. When Henry heard about that, Catherine wasn't allowed to leave her rooms anymore. Later she was sent to the Tower and executed, just like Anne Boleyn before her.

Henry's sixth and last wife was Catherine Parr. She was a rich widow who had been married twice before she accepted to become Henry's wife in 1543. Perhaps she too might have lost her head because of her religious ideas that were very different from Henry's, but she was clever enough not to turn Henry against her. She helped him to reconcile[14)] with his daughters Lady Mary and Lady Elizabeth, and the English parliament put them in the line of succession[15)] after his son Edward.

King Henry died on 28 January 1547, only 55 years old. Nine year old Edward became king, but he died after only six years on the throne. Now Henry's eldest daughter Mary became the first queen of England in 1553. After her death Henry's second daughter Elizabeth succeeded Mary in 1558.

1) Norman – normannisch (aus der Normandie in Nordfrankreich stammend)
2) unique – einzigartig
3) heir – Erbe
4) to refuse – ablehnen, verweigern
5) to excommunicate = exkommunizieren (aus der Kirche ausschließen)
6) to court sb. – jmd. umwerben
7) to get rid of sb. – jmd. loswerden
8) to accuse sb. – jmd. beschuldigen
9) mistress – Geliebte
10) Lord Chancellor – Lordkanzler, wichtigster königlicher Beamter und Berater
11) nonetheless – dennoch, trotzdem
12) to annul – annullieren, für ungültig erklären
13) court – königlicher Hof
14) to reconcile – sich versöhnen
15) line of succession – Thronfolge

Let's check

In den folgenden Übungen kannst du zeigen, wie gut du den Text verstanden hast. Während der Bearbeitung der einzelnen Aufgaben solltest du deine Lösungen immer mit dem Text vergleichen.

1. Matching sentences

Match the parts of the sentences correctly, then match the numbers with the letters in the small list below.

1	King Henry's first wife	a	was executed.
2	Henry wanted to divorce her because	b	had two husbands before Henry.
3	The pope in Rome	c	became king of England.
4	Then the pope excommunicated him and he	d	was the love of his life.
5	His second wife	e	couldn't produce a male heir either.
6	His third wife	f	was first married to his brother Arthur.
7	His fourth wife	g	founded the Church of England.
8	Like his second wife his fifth wife	h	was a German princess.
9	Wife number six	i	she couldn't give him a male heir.
10	After Henry's death his son Edward	j	refused to grant[1] Henry a divorce.

1	2	3	4	5	6	7	8	9	10

2. A summary of the text

Write the correct sentences from No. 1 in your exercise book. After each sentence add an extra sentence from the list below.

He made himself head of this new church.
She was a Spanish princess. ✔
She had an affair with Henry's servant.
But nonetheless he married his second wife.
They married in 1543.
She had a daughter who later became the first queen of England.
He was only nine years old.
She was accused of a love affair with her own brother and was executed.
But she died after she had given birth to a son.
Henry annulled their marriage after six months.

Example: Henry's first wife was first married to Henry's brother Arthur.
She was a Spanish princess.
Henry wanted to divorce her because …
She had a daughter …

1) to grant – gewähren, Erlaubnis erteilen, bewilligen

3. Who was it?

This person …

a) was the child of Henry's mistress: ______

b) had a love affair with the king's servant: ______

c) had different religious ideas: ______

d) didn't want to be touched by the king: ______

e) didn't accept that Henry divorced her: ______

f) died after childbirth: ______

g) was Henry's second child: ______

h) couldn't be king of England: ______

i) died in 1547: ______

j) died at the age of 15: ______

k) invaded England in 1066: ______

l) was Henry's second wife: ______

4. Questions on the text

Find the passages in the text that help you to answer the following questions. Underline them. In your answers you can use parts of the text, too.

a) Why was it so important to Henry to have a son?

______

b) What did Henry do after the pope had excommunicated him?

______

c) Why was Henry so disappointed in Anne Boleyn?

______

d) Why was Anne Boleyn executed?

______

e) Why did Henry not want to marry again after the death of Jane Seymour?

______

f) Was Edward Henry's only son?

______

g) Why did Henry marry Anne of Cleves?

______

h) Why did Henry often invite Anne of Cleves to court?

______

i) Why could Mary and Elizabeth become queens of England?

______

September 11, 2001

When Ron Cooper went to work on the morning of September 11, 2001 he didn't know that he was going to witness[1] one of the biggest catastrophes in American history.
Ron owned a small newspaper shop not far from the World Trade Center in Manhattan, New York City. Only minutes after he had opened his shop at 7.45 am a group of terrorists kidnapped two Boeing 767 at Logan Airport in Boston with more than 150 passengers on board.
Between 08.00 and 09.00 am Ron usually had a lot of customers. They bought newspapers, cigarettes, hot drinks or sweets, and many of them worked on the 110 floors[2] of the Twin[3] Towers, which were 411 m tall each. They were amongst[4] the tallest buildings in the world. On the morning of September 11, 2001 about 17,400 people were already working in their offices when the catastrophe took its course[5].

The towers of the WTC before the attack.

At 08.48 am the first Boeing crashed into the north tower and destroyed[6] about 18 floors. All the passengers on the plane and most of the people who worked between the 91st and the 107th floor were killed.
Shortly after the crash Ron ran out of his shop. The people in the street were watching the north tower. There were explosions, and smoke was coming out of a big hole in the upper floors. At first everybody believed that it was a terrible accident.
Then, at 09.02 am, the second Boeing crashed into the south tower above[7] the 77th floor.

There were more explosions. The upper floors of both towers were burning. Ron and all the other people who witnessed the catastrophe knew that the towers had been attacked. Fire engines arrived and firemen ran into the buildings. They tried to get to the upper floors. Everybody feared that there would be hundreds of injured[8] or dead people. And they were right. Thousands of people tried to get out of the buildings. But many doors were blocked, walls had collapsed, some of the stairwells[9] were destroyed, and most of the lifts were not working anymore.

The second plane crashes into the south tower.

Many people who had survived[10] on the upper floors escaped[11] onto the roofs. But because of the smoke the helicopters could not land there. More than 50 people died after they jumped out of the window. Hundreds of people phoned their friends and families. For most of them it was the last time.

Then, at 09.59 am, Ron couldn't believe his eyes when the south tower collapsed. Half an hour later, at 10.28 am, the north tower collapsed, too. The towers crashed into the streets of New York and destroyed most buildings next to them. Ron didn't see the collapse of the second tower. Like everybody else who was watching he ran for his life when the first tower collapsed in order not to[12] be killed by the falling rubble[13].

These people survived the horror.

Most of Manhattan was covered with thick grey dust. Ron survived. When he came home, he learned that not only the World Trade Center had been destroyed. Terrorists had also attacked the Pentagon in Arlington, Virginia, with another kidnapped plane. A fourth plane crashed in Pennsylvania before it could reach Washington, probably to attack the White House. On September 11, 2001 nearly 3,000 people died, about 2,700 of them in the World Trade Center. Only 1,570 dead bodies could be identified. Most of the others were never found. Ron's newspaper shop was not destroyed. But it was full of dust, and he had lost all his goods[14]. But worst of all was that he would never see so many of his customers again.

1) to witness – Zeuge sein, miterleben
2) floor – Stockwerk
3) twin – Zwilling(s-)
4) amongst – unter
5) to take its course – seinen/ihren Lauf nehmen
6) to destroy – zerstören
7) above – oberhalb von
8) injured – verletzt
9) stairwell – Treppenhaus
10) to survive – überleben
11) to escape – flüchten, entkommen
12) in order (not) to – um (nicht) zu
13) rubble – Trümmer
14) goods – Ware

Let's check

In den folgenden Übungen kannst du zeigen, wie gut du den Text verstanden hast. Während der Bearbeitung der einzelnen Aufgaben solltest du deine Lösungen immer mit dem Text vergleichen.

1. Right – wrong – not in the text?

		right	wrong	not in the text
a)	Ron Cooper worked in the World Trade Center.		X	
b)	Terrorists kidnapped two planes at Boston airport.	X		
c)	On September 11, 2001 Ron had about a hundred customers between 8.00 and 9.00 am.			X
d)	"World Trade Center" was the name of two tall buildings.			X
e)	Until 2001 the towers of the WTC were the tallest in the world.			
f)	When the first plane crashed into the north tower, 50,000 people died.			
g)	Most people who witnessed the first crash thought it was an accident.			
h)	Many people couldn't get out of the buildings because doors were blocked.			
i)	The people who escaped on the roof were rescued by helicopters.			
j)	Only four people survived when they jumped out of the windows.			
k)	Ron watched both towers collapse.			
l)	The dust that covered Manhattan was 20 centimetres thick.			
m)	On September 11, 2001 four planes were kidnapped.			
n)	Nearly 3,000 people died in the World Trade Center.			

2. Questions on the text

Write full answers. Remember to use the simple past.

a) What happened on September 11, 2001 at 08.42 and 09.02 am?

Two planes crashed

b) What can you say about the Twin Towers?

c) What did Ron Cooper usually sell to his customers?

d) What did the people who watched the first crash think?

e) Why could so many people not get out of the buildings?

f) Why did the people who escaped onto the roofs die?

g) What did about 50 people do because they couldn't get out of the buildings?

h) What happened to the Twin Towers?

i) Why did Ron survive September 11, 2001?

j) Why did the fourth kidnapped plane not reach Washington?

3. Can you get it right?

In the following sentences there are some mistakes. Can you spot them? Underline and correct them.

a) On the morning of September 11, 2001 one of the biggest earthquakes took place in American history. ______________________

b) Ron Cooper had a little café in Manhattan. ______________________

c) The Twin Towers were amongst the oldest buildings in the world. ______________________

d) When the first plane crashed, most people between the 91st and the 107th floor were injured. ______________________

e) At 09.20 am the second plane crashed into the south tower. ______________________

f) Policemen ran into the burning buildings. ______________________

g) Because of the heavy fog helicopters could not land on the roofs. ______________________

h) Ron saw the collapse of the second tower. ______________________

i) People ran for their lives because they didn't want to be killed by the explosions. ______________________

j) Ron's shop was full of rubble from the collapse of the Twin Towers. ______________________

4. Find the right order of the following sentences.

☐ The second plane crashed into the south tower at 09.02 am.

☐ But a lot of people couldn't get out of the buildings.

☐ Half an hour later the second tower collapsed.

☐ Not long after that two Boeing were kidnapped at Logan Airport in Boston.

☐ Firemen entered the buildings and tried to get to the upper floors.

[1] On September 11, 2001 Ron opened his newspaper shop at quarter to eight.

☐ There were explosions and fires in both towers.

☐ Because of the dust, Ron lost all his goods.

☐ But most of Manhattan was covered in thick dust.

☐ Others jumped out of the windows.

☐ People ran for their lives in order not to be killed by the rubble.

☐ At 09.59 the south tower collapsed.

☐ At 08.48 am the first plane crashed into the north tower.

☐ They all died.

☐ At that time about 17,400 people were in the buildings.

☐ The people who saw the crash thought it was an accident.

The sinking of the Titanic

April 10, 1912 was the most exciting day in Nora Murphy's life. The fourteen year old girl was standing with her eight year old sister Kate at the railing[1] of the *Titanic*, the biggest passenger ship in the world. Southampton and the south coast of England were quickly disappearing. The safest ship ever built was on her maiden voyage[2] to New York.

Three months earlier her dad had died in a coal-pit[3] accident in Wigan, a coal-mining town in the northwest of England. With the insurance[4] money from the mining company, and the money they got for their furniture and other belongings, her mother had bought three third-class tickets on the *Titanic*. They wanted to start a new life in Philadelphia where mum's sister Ann had been living with her family for six years.

For the following seven days they would share a cabin on G deck just above sea level with the Skoogs, another family of three from Birmingham. Nora and Kate had already made friends with the Skoog children Mabel and Elizabeth, and mum was glad that she had found a new friend in Mrs Skoog. The families enjoyed the first four days of the journey. The children played games on the poopdeck[5] or played cards in the common room. Sometimes Nora read from a story book to the smaller children while Mrs Skoog and mum knitted[6] and talked about their plans for America.

Third-class passengers had to stay on their decks. Locked gates leading up from the third-class section stopped third-class passengers from entering the upper class decks.

On Sunday night, April 14, at 11.35 pm Kate suddenly woke up. For dinner they had had herring and potatoes. The fish had been very salty, and now Kate was thirsty, but there was nothing to drink in their cabin. She woke Nora. 'Nora, I'm so thirsty. I need a drink.' Nora had an idea. – 'Look, Kate', she said. 'Let's try our dining-room. Perhaps there's still somebody there who can give you a drink. Otherwise we'll try the restaurant on B Deck.' – 'But that restaurant is only for the posh[7] people. They won't serve us', Kate protested. 'Let's see', Nora said. 'They cannot send a thirsty little girl away.' Cautiously[8] the girls left their cabin. They didn't want to wake up their mum, who hadn't been well all evening. Nora was glad that she was sleeping now.

Slowly the girls moved along the corridor towards the third-class dining room. Suddenly they heard a strange grinding sound,[9] and the ship trembled[10] for a few seconds. 'What was that?' Kate asked. 'I don't know' Nora answered, 'but it was a really strange noise.' 'I'm frightened, Nora. Let's go back to mum.' – 'Don't worry, Kate. It was probably nothing. Come on, let's find something to drink for you.'

The door to the dining-room was locked, so the girls went back to look for a staircase which would take them up to the restaurant on B deck. After about ten minutes they finally found it.

When they had gone up two flights of stairs they saw people standing in the corridor outside their cabins. They too had felt the sudden trembling of the *Titanic*. Then two men came quickly up the stairs from below. One of them shouted, 'Water, water's coming in! The lower decks are flooding quickly.' Then they ran past the girls. More people gathered in the corridor. 'Kate, we must find mum and warn her', Nora said. The girls began to go downstairs again. But they didn't get far. More people came up the stairs and blocked their way. A woman ran into Kate, and she fell on the stairs. Then a boy almost stepped on her. Kate began to cry, and a young man helped her to get up. Nora recognized him as another passenger on G deck. He shouted, 'Hurry up, girls. The ship is flooding. Let's get out of here.' – 'But we must find our mum,' Nora cried. 'You can't go downstairs now. G deck is flooding. My name's Patrick. Come on, I'll help you upstairs. I'm sure your mum will find you soon.' Then he lifted Kate on his arm and continued his way upstairs to the upper decks. Nora didn't know what to do. She wanted to find her mother, but she didn't want to lose her sister either[11]. More people were rushing upstairs, blocking her way downstairs. Nora finally decided to follow Patrick and Kate.

After two more flights of stairs the crowd suddenly came to a halt. Someone shouted, 'Open the gate and let us out.' Some people started to rattle and kick at the gate. Nora forced her way upstairs until she reached Patrick who was still carrying Kate. He was standing at the closed gate which was guarded by a steward. The steward shouted, 'Go back down to your quarters. There is no danger. The captain has everything under control.' Patrick put down Kate and said, 'The lower decks are flooding. So open the gate and let us out!' When the steward didn't react, Patrick signaled to another man who was also standing close to the gate. They started to kick against the gate until it fell into the corridor with a loud crash. The steward couldn't do anything and hastily stepped aside. Patrick took Nora and Kate by their hands and together with the other third-class passengers they went out on the promenade deck. The night air was cold, and the girls started to shiver because they were only wearing their night dresses. Women and children were running and shouting. Many were wearing life vests[12]. They passed a man who was talking to a woman. 'Don't worry, my dear. This ship has a very special construction. It is unsinkable.' Yes, Nora had heard that, too. Could such a big and wonderful ship like the *Titanic* really sink? Still she did not know what had happened that could make the ship sink. Then she saw a steward. He was helping a lady into a life vest. Nora stopped and asked, 'Sir, please, can you tell me what has happened?' The steward turned to Nora and said, 'The *Titanic* hit an iceberg. We're sinking.' Then he concentrated on the lady again. Kate was crying again, 'I want my mum. I want my mum.' Nora took her in her arms. 'Don't worry. She'll come soon and find us.' Patrick led the girls to some deckchairs[13]. 'Sit down and wait here,' he said. 'I'll fetch some life vests for you.' Then he disappeared. A band was playing a waltz. Nora thought that this was very strange. How can people play music on a sinking ship? Nora saw that the bow[14] of the *Titanic* had already sunk. She was very worried about her mum now. Their cabin was near the bow. It was probably flooded with icy water by now. After a while Patrick came back with two life vests. He had found seats in a lifeboat for the girls, too. 'Come on, girls. We must get you into a lifeboat.' Patrick and the girls fought their way along the upper deck to one of the lifeboats. About thirty women and children were sitting in it. There was still plenty of room. An officer was shouting at a man who wanted to enter the lifeboat. 'You can't get in. It's women and children first.' Patrick lifted Kate into the boat, but Nora didn't want to follow her sister. She was still looking for her mum. The officer who was watching them got angry and shouted at Nora, 'Get in that boat at once. We haven't got all night.' He took her by her arms and almost threw her into the boat which was already lowering[15] towards the sea below. Nora couldn't see Patrick anymore. He had disappeared, too. She couldn't even say good-bye to him. Nora shouted, 'Wait, the boat is not full yet. Our mum is still on the ship. Can't we wait for her?' 'Shut up', the seaman who was with them in the lifeboat shouted. 'There are many other boats. We must get away from here.'

The boat hit the North Atlantic. Kate was still crying. Nora tried to comfort[16] her. 'Don't worry. Mum will make it. She'll be in another boat. You'll see.' A lady took off her coat and gave it to the sisters. Nora wrapped it around Kate and herself, and at once they felt a lot warmer. The seaman took the oars[17] and rowed the boat away from the *Titanic*. Now Nora saw other lifeboats. Like their boat most of them were only half full with people, but Nora hoped their mum would be in one of them. Nobody in the lifeboat talked. Everybody watched the *Titanic* sink lower and lower at the bow and listened to the panicking people who were still on board.

Suddenly the lights went out in the bow of the *Titanic*. From their lifeboat they could hear the band play again, and the hundreds of people who were still on board began to sing *Nearer my God to thee*. It was a very emotional moment, and some of the other women in the boat started to cry.

Suddenly there was a great noise. Then the stern[18] began to rise out of the water. It slowly lifted high into the air. It stayed there for about half a minute. Many people were either jumping or falling from the ship. Slowly first, then quicker and quicker the stern sank into the water and vanished[19]. It was 02.20 am on April 15, 1912.

Nora would never forget the terrible screams of the dying people when the ship sank. She would never forget the hundreds of dead bodies that were floating[20] in the water later. And she would never forget her mum who was one of the 1,503 people who had died.

The next morning, the liner *Carpathia* rescued the 705 survivors and took them to New York. Nora and Kate were expected by their aunt Ann who took care of them.

1) railing – Reling
2) maiden voyage – Jungfernfahrt
3) coal-pit – Kohlenmine
4) insurance – Versicherung
5) poopdeck – offenes Deck am Heck
6) to knit – stricken
7) posh – vornehm
8) cautious – vorsichtig
9) grinding sound – mahlendes Geräusch
10) to tremble – zittern
11) not … either – auch nicht
12) life vest – Schwimmweste
13) deckchair – Liegestuhl
14) bow – Schiffsbug
15) to lower – senken
16) to comfort sb. – jmd. trösten, beruhigen
17) oar – Ruder
18) stern – Schiffsheck
19) to vanish – verschwinden
20) to float – treiben

Let's check

In den folgenden Übungen kannst du zeigen, wie gut du den Text verstanden hast. Während der Bearbeitung der einzelnen Aufgaben solltest du deine Lösungen immer mit dem Text vergleichen.

1. Right – wrong – not in the text?

	right	wrong	not in the text
a) The *Titanic* disaster happened on her first voyage to America.			
b) The Murphys left England because Mr Murphy had lost his job in a coal-pit.			
c) Third-class passengers often had to share their cabins with other families.			
d) Gates separated the different classes on board.			
e) Kate woke up because she heard a grinding sound.			
f) It was a very long way from the girls' cabin to the third-class dining room.			
g) After the collision with the iceberg the lower decks soon began to flood.			
h) Nora and Kate couldn't go back to their cabin because they had lost their way.			
i) Patrick was a coal miner from Wigan.			
j) A steward didn't want to open the gate to the promenade deck.			
k) Nora hoped that her mother would find her and Kate.			
l) Patrick entered the lifeboat with the girls.			
m) The girls' mother was in one of the other life boats.			
n) Before the ship sank, the people on board sang a religious song.			
o) Many people died after they had jumped or fallen into the water when the ship sank.			
p) The *Carpathia* did not have enough cabins for the survivors.			

2. Please correct the sentences that are wrong in No. 1. *(There are five.)*

____

____

____

____

____

3. Questions on the text

a) Why did the Murphys leave England? _______________

b) What had happened to Mr Murphy? _______________

c) How could Mrs Murphy pay for the tickets? _______________

d) Why were there gates on the *Titanic*? _______________

e) What happened when Nora and Kate were on their way to their dining room? _______________

f) Why could the girls not warn their mother? _______________

g) What did Nora learn from a steward on the promenade deck? _______________

h) What did Nora find very strange? _______________

i) Why did a lady in the lifeboat give her coat to the girls? _______________

j) What happened before the *Titanic* finally sank? _______________

4. Write a summary of the text.

(Remember: The text is written in the simple past. Your summary must be written in the simple past, too.)

- April 10, 1912 / *Titanic* / maiden voyage / Southampton to New York
- Nora, Kate and Mrs Murphy / third-class cabin / Skoog family
- start new life / Nora's and Kate's aunt / Philadelphia
- April 14 / 11.35 pm / Kate wake up / thirsty
- Nora and Kate / find something to drink / dining-room
- suddenly / hear / grinding sound / tremble
- door to dining-room closed / go upstairs to restaurant on B deck
- after two flights of stairs / people from lower decks / run upstairs / lower decks flooding
- Kate and Nora / can't warn mother / more people / upstairs / block way
- young man / help / promenade deck
- young man / find life vests / two seats in lifeboat
- Nora / hope / mother / in another lifeboat
- April 15 / 02.20 am / sink
- 1,503 people die / among them mother
- *Carpathia* / rescue 705 survivors / take them to New York

Start like this:

On April 10, 1912, the Titanic started on her maiden voyage from Southampton to New York.

Please go on.

5. Read between the lines.

a) Why could the third-class passengers only go on the poopdeck instead of the promenade deck on one of the upper decks?

____

____

b) Why did many people believe that the *Titanic* was unsinkable?

____

____

c) Why did the band play almost until the *Titanic* sank?

____

____

d) Why were many of the lifeboats not full?

____

____

The big earthquake[1]

On the morning of March 11, 2011 Ayaka Sato awoke with a sore throat and a runny nose. She hadn't slept much that night and didn't feel too well. Her mum decided that Ayaka would not go to school that day but stay in bed instead. Both her parents had to go to work and there was nobody who could look after Ayaka. But she was almost 12 years old, so her mum thought she could stay on her own until she came back in the afternoon. She prepared[2] some steamed[3] rice and miso soup[4] for her daughter and left the food on the kitchen table. Ayaka could warm it up in the microwave oven when she was hungry.

The Satos lived in a small new house near the sea on the outskirts[5] of Natori City in the north-east of Honshu, the biggest island of Japan. Momoka, Ayaka's mum, worked as shop assistant in a department store in the city centre, and Haruki, her dad, was the manager of a big computer shop.

After her parents had left, Ayaka got up and had something to eat and drink. She went back to her bed and switched on her TV. But after some time she was bored with the comedy shows and the soaps and soon fell asleep.

She woke up when her bed was shaking violently[6]. Ayaka knew at once that this was an earthquake. There had been smaller earthquakes before, but this one was really big. Quickly she crawled under her bed. At school she had learned that in case of an earthquake the most important thing was to seek shelter[7]. The shaking didn't stop. She could hear plates, cups, and pots fall off the kitchen shelf, and the smaller pieces of furniture were moving. Suddenly the shelf in her room crashed next to her bed. Now it would be more difficult for her to free herself from under her bed. Ayaka hoped that the ceiling[8] would not come down on her bed, too.

After about five long minutes the earthquake was over. The house was quiet now, and Ayaka was very frightened and cold. She had to phone her parents. Where was her mobile? Her mum had put it on her bedside table before she left.

Ayaka tried to move the shelf that had fallen right next to her, but she was too weak. She shouted for help, again and again.

Suddenly she heard a noise. Someone was inside the house. 'Hello, Mrs Sato, Mr Sato, Ayaka, are you here?' That was Mr Ito, their next door neighbour, and Ayaka felt a great relief[9]. 'In here', she shouted, 'in my bedroom.'

A few moments later Mr Ito moved the shelf and helped Ayaka out from under her bed. She looked around. The house was a total mess. There were piles[10] of household items[11] and pieces of furniture. 'Quick', Mr Ito said. 'We must get out of here. This isn't over yet.' 'But I must call my parents and ask them how they are', Ayaka protested. 'No, Ayaka. There is no time. We can do that later. Come on now.'

Mr Ito grabbed Ayaka's left arm and dragged[12] her out of the house which no longer had a front door.

Mr Ito ran with Ayaka to his car which was standing next to his house or what was left of it. The windows were broken, and part of the roof had come down. Mrs Ito and her two little children were already sitting in the car. Mr Ito put Ayaka on the back seat next to his children and started the engine.

Then Mrs Ito screamed, 'Look, the water is coming! Let's get away!' Everybody looked in the direction of the sea. A big wave[13] of water was coming towards them. 'Oh no, it's a tsunami', Ayaka thought. Mr Ito was already driving on the quayside[14]. The water was coming quickly. Another three hundred yards and they would reach the road junction[15]. Fortunately there was not much traffic. Mr Ito turned left and drove faster. Ayaka turned round and looked out of the rear window[16].

The big earthquake

The 20 foot[17] wave had reached the quayside and crashed on the first houses. Only seconds later they were completely destroyed. There were loud explosions and fires. Some cars that were coming behind them were swallowed[18] by the water. The water was too quick. But the Itos got away. 'Where are we going?', Ayaka asked after they had driven without speaking for another five minutes. 'To my sister's,' Mrs Ito answered. 'She lives north of Natori, and the wave can't reach it. Suddenly Ayaka remembered her parents again. 'But I must contact my parents', she said. 'They will be very worried.' Mrs Ito gave Ayaka her mobile. Her mum answered after the first ring. She was very excited. 'Ayaka, where are you? We tried your mobile, but it was dead.' 'I'm with the Itos. We are going to see Mrs Ito's sister.' 'Oh, I'm so glad. Stay there. We will pick you up as soon as we can.' Ayaka asked, 'Mum, are you and dad okay?' 'Yes, darling, don't worry. Dad and I were having a drink in the restaurant on the 5th floor of my department store when the earthquake started. Now the streets are flooded because of the tsunami. We can't get out yet.'

Two days later Mr and Mrs Sato picked up their daughter. They thanked the Itos. When Ayaka said good-bye to Mr Ito she asked him, 'How did you know that the tsunami was coming when you saved me from our house, Mr Ito?' 'Well, the night before the earthquake there was a report about earthquakes and tsunamis on TV. So when the earthquake started I put two and two together.'

With a magnitude[19] of 8.9 the earthquake was one of the biggest ever in Japan. Because of the earthquake and the tsunami about 15,800 people lost their lives. More than 3,700 people are still missing.

1) earthquake – Erdbeben
2) to prepare – vorbereiten
3) steamed – gedämpft
4) miso soup – Suppe aus Fischsud und Sojabohnenpaste (jap. Nationalgericht)
5) outskirts – Außenbereich, Vorort
6) violent – heftig, stark
7) to seek shelter – Schutz suchen
8) ceiling – Zimmerdecke
9) relief – Erleichterung
10) pile – Haufen
11) household items – Haushaltsgegenstände
12) to drag – (mit)reißen, ziehen
13) wave – Welle
14) quayside – Uferstraße
15) road junction – Straßenkreuzung
16) rear window – Heckscheibe
17) foot – Fuß (engl./am. Längenmaß: 1 foot (ft) = 0,3048 m)
18) to swallow – (ver)schlucken
19) magnitude – Erdbebenstärke

Let's check

In den folgenden Übungen kannst du zeigen, wie gut du den Text verstanden hast. Während der Bearbeitung der einzelnen Aufgaben solltest du deine Lösungen immer mit dem Text vergleichen.

1. Which ending/s fit/s best?

Compare with the text. Sometimes more than one ending is correct.

1. Ayaka Sato didn't go to school, because
   - ☐ a) her mother didn't feel well.
   - ☐ b) she didn't feel well.
   - ☐ c) she had a sore throat.

2. Mrs Sato prepared some food for Ayaka
   - ☐ a) so she could eat it when she was hungry.
   - ☐ b) because she was already 12 years old.
   - ☐ c) because her parents went to work.

3. Ayaka woke up
   - ☐ a) when she was hungry.
   - ☐ b) because she had forgotten to switch off the TV.
   - ☐ c) when the earthquake started.

4. Ayaka was frightened, because
   - ☐ a) the earthquake lasted for five minutes.
   - ☐ b) she didn't know what to do.
   - ☐ c) she couldn't find her mobile.

5. Mr Ito came into the Satos' house
   - ☐ a) after the earthquake.
   - ☐ b) because he thought that the Satos needed help.
   - ☐ c) because he wanted to kidnap Ayaka.

6. The Itos wanted to get away quickly
   - ☐ a) because Ayaka needed a doctor.
   - ☐ b) because a tsunami was coming.
   - ☐ c) because there was not much traffic.

7. The wave
   - ☐ a) destroyed the houses along the quayside.
   - ☐ b) was closely behind the Itos' car.
   - ☐ c) was more than 20 foot high.

8. Mr and Mrs Sato
   - ☐ a) survived the catastrophe in a department store.
   - ☐ b) were worried about Ayaka.
   - ☐ c) couldn't find their daughter after the tsunami.

2. Questions on the text

Find the passages in the text that help you to answer the following questions. Underline them. In your answers you can use parts of the text, too.

a) Why didn't Ayaka go to school on March 11, 2011? (*Find four facts.*)

____

____

b) What were Mr and Mrs Sato's jobs?

____

____

c) Why did Ayaka crawl under her bed when the earthquake started?

____

____

d) Why was Ayaka worried during the earthquake? *(Find two facts.)*

____

____

e) Why didn't Mr Ito allow Ayaka to call her parents?

____

____

f) What could Ayaka see out of the rear window of Mr Ito's car?

____

____

g) Why did the Itos want to go to Mrs Ito's sister's?

____

____

h) Why did Mr and Mrs Sato survive the tsunami?

____

____

i) Why did Mr Ito know that the earthquake was not the only catastrophe?

____

____

3. Write a summary of the text.

(Remember: The text is written in the simple past. Your summary must be written in the simple past, too.)

- March 11, 2011 / not go to school / not feel well
- mother / prepare some food / eat / be hungry
- Mr and Mrs Sato / go to work
- something to eat and drink / watch TV / fall asleep
- wake up / earthquake / crawl under bed
- shelf / crash / difficult to free
- neighbour Mr Ito / help / run out of house / push into car
- big wave from the seaside / but drive fast / escape
- call parents / survive in department store / worried
- two days later / pick up / Mrs Ito's sister's

Start like this:

On March 11, 2011 Ayaka Sato didn't go to school because she didn't feel well.

____

____

____

____

____

____

____

____

____

____

4. Find an expression in the text for …

a) a symptom of a cold: ______________________

b) an area outside a town: ______________________

c) the opposite of strong: ______________________

d) a person who lives next door: ______________________

e) things: ______________________

f) a road along the sea: ______________________

g) very strong and with the power to destroy: ______________________

h) bedside table, shelf, bed …: ______________________

Stop bullying me

On her first day at her new school in Birmingham Valerie didn't know that it would be the beginning of a nightmare[1].

She had moved with her parents from a small village in Wales because her dad had found a new job in Birmingham. At her old school she had a lot of friends, and the teachers were okay. So she was very sad when she left.

Her new school was big, and she felt frightened with so many pupils. Mrs Watson, her new form teacher, introduced[2] Valerie to her new class. 'This is Valerie. She moved from Wales to Birmingham. Please make her feel welcome.'

At lunch break Valerie already knew that some of the girls of her new class would not welcome her at all. She was having lunch in the school cafeteria when Brenda, Sue, and Miranda came to her table. 'Hello, village girl', Brenda said. 'Tell us about your life as a cowgirl in Wales.' Valerie didn't know what to say. She was too shy and suddenly afraid of the three girls. So she simply stood up, left her lunch on the table, and ran out of the cafeteria. Outside she began to cry, but she was careful that nobody noticed[3].

The following weeks Brenda and her gang didn't leave Valerie alone. Between lessons they pinched[4] her exercise books and tore out[5] her homework. During lunch breaks they followed her to the cafeteria, sat at her table, and dropped her food to the floor. After school on their way home they called her names like cowgirl, plain Jane,[6] and baby face. They punched[7] and kicked her, and one rainy day they even took her jacket away.

Valerie didn't tell her parents about her problems. Her dad worked hard in his new job and often came home late. Her mum was looking for a job, too. So she often was out for job interviews when Valerie came home. Valerie didn't talk to Mrs Watson, either. She was frightened that the girls would bully her even more if she said anything.

Sometimes Valerie asked Brenda, Sue, and Miranda to stop bullying her, but they only laughed and punched her even harder. The other pupils of her class who sometimes saw or heard what the bullies were doing to Valerie never said or did anything to help her. They didn't want to be the gang's next victims[8]. Valerie stopped going to the cafeteria and lost weight. She didn't do her homework, so the bullies couldn't tear it out of her exercise books. She had bad marks in her tests, and Mrs Watson asked her what was wrong with her. Valerie answered that everything was fine and that she had only been too lazy to study for the tests.

One day Mrs Watson left her handbag in the classroom next to her desk. Brenda saw it first. She went to Valerie's table and said, 'I think we could stop bullying you. We could even be friends.' There was hope in Valerie's voice when she said, 'Yes, it would be really nice if you stopped doing all those nasty[9] things to me.' 'Sure, cowgirl', Brenda answered. 'But you must earn it.' 'Earn it?' 'Yes, sweetie. See that bag next to the desk? Go and pinch Mrs Watson's purse!'

'What?', Valerie shouted. 'No, I won't do that. I'm no thief.'

'Okay, if you don't do it, you will suffer[10] for it', Brenda whispered into Valerie's ear.

'No', Valerie shouted again. 'That's enough now.'

Everybody looked at her. Valerie went on, 'You and your gang have bullied me since I first came here. I've never told anybody, and no one in this class has ever helped me. But I'm no thief!'

Now Brenda hit Valerie in the face. 'Shut up, you stupid cow, or you'll regret[11] it.'

'Very interesting to watch and listen to you, Brenda,' a woman's voice suddenly said. It was Mrs Watson. She had come back to fetch her handbag. Nobody saw her entering the classroom, but she had heard everything that Valerie and Brenda had said.

'I always had that feeling that you meant mischief[12], Brenda. And now I know I was right', she said. 'You will feel sorry for what you've done to Valerie. I'll see to that. Perhaps you will even have to leave this school.'

Now Valerie said, 'I'm glad everything is coming out and I'm sorry I didn't talk to anybody about what Brenda and her gang did to me. I know that was a mistake. I will leave this school as soon as my parents find another one for me. And I hope that my classmates there won't look away when someone is bullied.' Valerie took her satchel[13] and her coat. Nobody said a word when she left the classroom.

1) nightmare – Alptraum
2) to introduce so. – jmd. vorstellen
3) to notice sth. – etw. bemerken
4) to pinch – klauen, mopsen
5) to tear sth. out (tore) – etwas herausreißen
6) plain Jane – unscheinbares Mädchen
7) to punch so. – jmd. mit der Faust schlagen
8) victim – Opfer
9) nasty – gemein, widerlich
10) to suffer – büßen, leiden
11) to regret – bereuen
12) to mean mischief – Böses im Schilde führen
13) satchel – Schultasche, Ranzen

Let's check

In den folgenden Übungen kannst du zeigen, wie gut du den Text verstanden hast. Während der Bearbeitung der einzelnen Aufgaben solltest du deine Lösungen immer mit dem Text vergleichen.

1. Right – wrong – not in the text?

		right	wrong	not in the text
a)	Valerie was pleased to leave her old home in Wales.		X	
b)	On her first day Valerie already knew that some girls didn't like her.	X		
c)	Brenda and her gang called Valerie names at the cafeteria.	X	X	
d)	Valerie started to cry in the cafeteria.		X	
e)	Life wasn't easy for her the following weeks.	X		
f)	She was ill after the gang had taken away her jacket.			X
g)	She didn't talk to her teacher because she was afraid of her.		X	
h)	The gang bullied her more when Valerie asked them to stop.	X		
i)	Her classmates didn't help her because they were afraid of the gang.	X		
j)	She stopped doing her homework because she was too lazy to do it.		X	
k)	Valerie would have been happy if the gang had stopped bullying her.	X		
l)	She wanted to steal the purse when Brenda said she would stop bullying her.		X	
m)	There was a lot of money in Mrs Watson's purse.			X
n)	Brenda threatened Valerie if she didn't steal the purse.	X		
o)	Mrs Watson was surprised when she heard Brenda talk to Valerie.		X	
p)	Valerie wants to leave her school.	X		

2. Please correct the sentences that are wrong in No. 1. *(There are six.)*

She was sad about it.
~~They called her name after school~~
She run out and looked for that nobody notice her cry. She was afraid of the gang.
No she stopped it because of the girls.
She never want to steal the bag
She already thought this.

3. Find an expression in the text for …

a) bad dreams: nightmare

b) stealing: ~~to~~ pinch

c) a person who threatens or hurts others: bully

d) a girl who has an average appearance: plain Jane

e) hitting somebody with your fists: to punch

f) someone who steals: thief

g) school bag: ~~hand bag~~ satchel

h) another pupil in your class: classmates

4. What did the bullies do?

Make a list of the things that Brenda and her gang did to Valerie. Write headwords (Stichpunkte).

______

______

______

______

______

______

5. How did Valerie react to the bullying? *(Find at least four things.)*

______

______

______

______

6. Read between the lines.

a) Find reasons why she didn't tell her parents about the bullies.

______

______

______

b) Find reasons why she didn't go to the cafeteria anymore after a while.

______

______

______

c) Find reasons why she had bad marks in her tests.

______

______

______

7. State your opinion.

What would you do if someone tried to bully you? *(Write at least three aspects.)*

______

______

______

______

______

______

The Aboriginal people of Australia

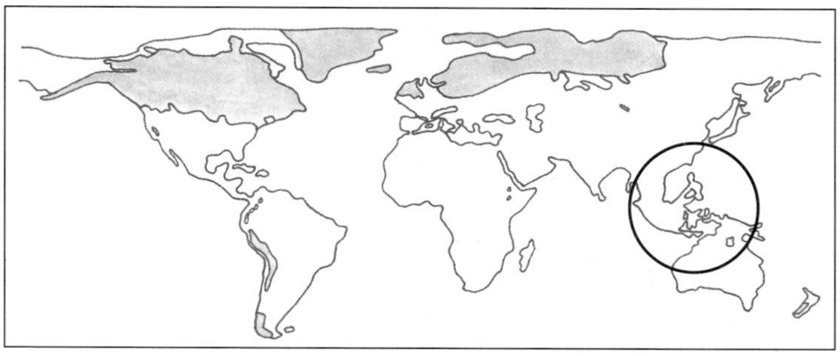

The word *Aborigine* comes from the Latin words *ab origine*. It means *the first* or *the earliest known*. It describes the native people who have always lived there. The word *Aborigines** was first used in 1770 by the first Europeans who settled[1] in Australia.
It is not quite clear where the first Aboriginals came from, but scientists[2] believe that they had come from Indonesia during the ice age about 40,000 to 60,000 years ago. At that time it was still possible to reach Australia on foot or by boat. Australia was joined to New Guinea, and the other Indonesian islands were larger than today, and the sea passages to Australia were smaller.
The Aboriginals mostly settled on the east coast of Australia because of the better climate. Some tribes[3] also settled in central Australia. They lived in harmony with nature and had no contact to the rest of the world. So they could not learn about new techniques, and they didn't trade goods[4].
There were 500 to 700 people in a tribe, but they usually lived in smaller groups of 20 to 50 people. Most of them were nomads, hunters, fishermen and gatherers[5]. They invented the returning boomerang that they used for hunting and the didgeridoo, the famous musical instrument made of wood.

When the European settlers arrived in Australia in 1770, between 300,000 to 1,000,000 Aboriginal people lived there. Today there are only about 550,000 Aboriginal people. The overall population of Australia is 23 million people.
The first Europeans didn't understand the Aboriginal culture and felt superior[6]. They thought it would be necessary to teach those "*savages*"[7] the superior British culture. They did inhuman and sadistic things to them. First they took away their land. They called it *terra nullius*, which means it didn't belong to anyone.
Then they discriminated and even enslaved[8] the Aboriginals. And when they were too old to work or became sick, their British masters didn't keep them but sent them away.
Aboriginals who were free were not allowed to vote[9] in general elections[10] until the early 20th century, and most of them could not read or write.
A terrible thing that the Europeans did to the Aboriginal people of Australia became known as the so-called *lost generation.*
Aboriginal children were taken away from their parents and put in foster homes[11] or special children's homes where they were taught British culture and lifestyle. With this method the British wanted to breed out[12] Aboriginal genes. This system finally finished in the 1970s. As a consequence many Aboriginal people living in Australia today don't know anything about their true families. Yet the Aboriginal culture which is over 40,000 years old is still alive although the British tried everything to destroy it.
The Aboriginals were given their civil rights[13] in 1967. From then on they were allowed to live wherever they wanted to. They still belong to the poorest part of the Australian population[14]. The 20% unemployment rate[15] is nearly three times higher than the unemployment rate of the average[16] population. Their education still isn't as good as that of other Australians, and they have fewer chances to well-paid careers. The crime rate is extremely high. Twenty per cent of all prisoners in Australian prisons are Aboriginal people.
In today's multicultural Australia where people with different cultural backgrounds from all over the world live, it's still difficult for the Aboriginals to find their place. But their special way of life and their cultural heritage[17] make people feel interested in the fifth continent and visit Australia.

* Inzwischen gilt das Wort „*Aborigine*" im Englischen als abwertend und wird durch „*Aboriginal*" ersetzt. Im Deutschen wird weiterhin der Begriff „*Aborigine*" verwendet.
1) to settle – ansiedeln
2) scientist – Wissenschaftler
3) tribe – Volksstamm
4) to trade goods – mit Waren handeln
5) gatherer – Sammler
6) superior – überlegen
7) savage – Wilder
8) to enslave – versklaven
9) to vote – wählen
10) election – Wahl
11) foster home – Pflegefamilie
12) to breed out – herauszüchten
13) civil rights – Bürgerrechte
14) population – Bevölkerung
15) unemployment rate – Arbeitslosenrate
16) average – Durchschnitts-
17) heritage – Erbe

Let's check

In den folgenden Übungen kannst du zeigen, wie gut du den Text verstanden hast. Während der Bearbeitung der einzelnen Aufgaben solltest du deine Lösungen immer mit dem Text vergleichen.

1. Right – wrong – not in the text?

		right	wrong	not in the text
a)	The name *Aborigines* was given to the Australian natives by European settlers.			
b)	During the ice-age it was still possible to get to Australia on foot.			
c)	The Aboriginals were always interested in trading things with other tribes.			
d)	Within a tribe 20 people were hunters.			
e)	When the Europeans arrived, about 380,000 Aboriginals lived in Australia.			
f)	About 3.5% of the Australian population are Aboriginals.			
g)	The Europeans liked and accepted the Aboriginal culture.			
h)	The Europeans decided that the Aboriginal land didn't belong to anybody.			
i)	Aboriginal slaves could stay with their masters until they died.			
j)	Until the early 20th century Aboriginal children went to school for only two years.			
k)	*Lost generation* is the name for taking away Aboriginal children from their families.			
l)	This method should help to destroy the Aboriginal culture.			
m)	Today Aboriginals have the same rights as other Australians.			
n)	Their education is as good as that of other Australians.			
o)	Australian prisons are mainly filled with Aboriginal people.			

2. Please correct the sentences that are wrong in No. 1. *(There are six.)*

3. Finish the sentences.

Read the text again and find meaningful endings. Sometimes there is more than one possibility.

a) The word *Aborigine (find 2 facts)*

b) The first Aboriginals

c) Most Aboriginal tribes settled

d) Within their bigger tribes they usually

e) The Aboriginals are still famous for

f) Between 300,000 and one million Aboriginals lived in Australia when

g) The Europeans felt superior to the Aboriginals and therefore they

h) The expression *terra nullius* means

i) Aboriginals who were not enslaved

j) The expression *lost generation* meant that

k) As a consequence many Aboriginals

l) Nowadays the Aboriginals *(find 2 facts)*

4. Explain in German.

Your little cousin is interested in the Aboriginals but he doesn't understand English. Explain to him in German.

a) Was bedeutet eigentlich Aborigine? ______________________

____

____

b) Woher kamen die Aborigines? ______________________

____

____

c) Wie haben die Aborigines früher gelebt? ______________________

____

____

d) Warum haben die europäischen Siedler die Aborigines zu ihren Sklaven gemacht? ______________________

____

____

e) Warum wurden viele Aborigine-Kinder ihren Familien weggenommen? ______________________

____

____

f) Warum sind viele Aborigines heute arm oder arbeitslos? ______________________

____

____

5. Find titles for the parts of the text.

Ordne die folgenden Überschriften den verschiedenen inhaltlichen Abschnitten des Textes zu und gib die jeweiligen Textzeilen an!

The lost generation – Early Aboriginal life in Australia – Aboriginal life in the 20th and 21st century – Where does the name Aborigine come from? – The European settlers feel superior

Line 1 to ____: ______________________

Line ____ to ____: ______________________

Line ____ to ____: ______________________

Line ____ to ____: ______________________

Line ____ to ____: ______________________

German Reunification[1)]

When the Second World War finally ended in 1945, the Allies[2)] (USA, the Soviet Union, Britain, and France) divided[3)] Germany and its capital Berlin into four occupation zones[4)].

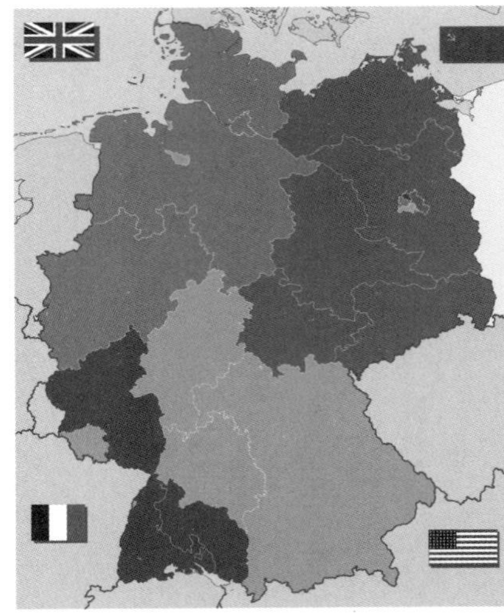

In 1949, the British, American, and French zones became the Federal Republic of Germany[5)] (West Germany), while the Soviet zone became the German Democratic Republic[6)] (East Germany). East Berlin became the capital of the GDR, and West Berlin remained part of West Germany. If people wanted to visit or leave the city, they had to travel on transit roads through Eastern German territory. The new capital of West Germany became Bonn, a small and quiet town on the river Rhine.

Both German states developed[7)] in different ways. The economy[8)] grew[9)] in the west. Within ten years the people had not only built new factories and created many new jobs but also lived in wealth[10)]. They built houses, bought cars, and enjoyed travelling to foreign countries such as Italy, Spain and Portugal.

The German Democratic Republic was a socialist state and was politically dependent upon[11)] the Soviet Union. The government organized the industrial production rates, the people did not have much private property, and there was not a lot they could buy in shops or at the markets. Although the GDR had the highest standard of living in the Eastern Bloc countries, about 2.7 million people escaped[12)] to the Federal Republic of Germany during the 1950s because they couldn't cope with the economic problems there.

In order to stop so many people from escaping from their country the Berlin Wall was built in 1961. Frontier barriers[13)] were constructed along the inter-German border which was controlled by soldiers on watch towers. It was one of the best guarded borders in the world. People who tried illegal migration to West Berlin or West Germany were often shot on the spot[14)]. The people of East Germany were imprisoned[15)] by their own government. If East Germans wanted to travel to other countries, they could only visit other socialist or communist states such as Poland, Czechoslovakia, Hungary, Bulgaria, or the Soviet Union.

In 1989 East Germans started to demonstrate against their government, beginning in the city of Leipzig. The demonstrations usually took place on a Monday, so they were known as the Monday demonstrations. Every Monday the number of demonstrators grew bigger. They carried banners and posters saying ***We are the people*** and demanding better living and travel conditions. In October 1989 the leader of the GDR, Erich Honecker, resigned,[16)] and Egon Krenz took over. Krenz promised democratic reforms and new regulations for trips to the West, but he also wanted to save the socialist regime.

On November 9, the government decided to allow East Germans to go to West Germany without an official permission. This was to begin in the afternoon of November 10. But the government spokesman was not well informed. At a press conference on the evening of November 9, he said that trips to West Germany were possible from that very moment on. At once thousands of East Germans went to the crossing points in East Berlin and made the officials open the barriers. Then they crossed into West Berlin for the first time.

People from both parts of the city even started to destroy part of the Wall that same night. It was a non-violent[17)] revolution, and neither the East German government nor the reformist leader of the Soviet Union, Mikhail Gorbachev, tried to stop the people from reuniting.

On October 3, 1990 both German states reunited officially. There are now sixteen federal states with Berlin as capital.

1) reunification – Wiedervereinigung
2) Allies – Verbündete
3 to divide – (auf)teilen
4) occupation zone – Besatzungszone
5) Federal Republic of Germany – Bundesrepublik Deutschland
6) German Democratic Republic – Deutsche Demokratische Republik
7) to develop – entwickeln
8) economy – Wirtschaft
9) to grow/grew – wachsen
10) wealth – Wohlstand
11) to be dependent upon – abhängig sein von
12) to escape – flüchten
13) frontier barrier – Grenzabsperrung
14) on the spot – sofort, auf der Stelle
15) to be imprisoned – gefangen sein
16) to resign – zurücktreten
17) non-violent – gewaltlos

Let's check

1. Which ending/s fit/s best?

Compare with the text. Sometimes more than one ending is correct.

1. When the Second World War ended,
   - ☐ a) Berlin became the capital of Germany.
   - ☒ b) Germany was divided into four occupation zones.
   - ☐ c) the Soviet zone became the German Democratic Republic.

2. In 1949, East Berlin
   - ☐ a) became the capital of the Soviet zone.
   - ☐ b) remained part of the Federal Republic of Germany.
   - ☒ c) became the capital of the GDR.

3. The Federal Republic of Germany
   - ☒ a) made Bonn its capital.
   - ☐ b) made West Berlin its capital.
   - ☐ c) developed differently than the GDR.

4. The German Democratic Republic
   - ☐ a) allowed its people to travel to Italy and Spain.
   - ☒ b) didn't allow its people a lot of private property.
   - ☐ c) made Bonn its capital.

5. During the 1950s
   - ☐ a) millions of people escaped the GDR.
   - ☒ b) the Berlin Wall was built.
   - ☐ c) Monday demonstrations took place in Leipzig.

6. Between the 1960s and 1980s
   - ☐ a) soldiers controlled the frontier from watch towers.
   - ☒ b) people who tried to escape from the GDR were often shot.
   - ☐ c) Eastern Germans could only visit socialist or communist states.

7. The Monday demonstrators
   - ☐ a) didn't want to travel to Poland, Czechoslovakia, or other socialist countries.
   - ☐ b) wanted better living conditions in their country.
   - ☒ c) grew in number every week.

8. On November 9, 1989
   - ☒ a) the barriers were opened because of a mistake made by the government spokesman.
   - ☐ b) many Eastern Germans came to West Berlin for the first time.
   - ☐ c) Erich Honecker resigned.

9. On October 3, 1990
   - ☐ a) Mikhail Gorbachev became leader of the Soviet Union.
   - ☐ b) sixteen new federal states were built.
   - ☒ c) both German parts officially became one country.

2. Finish the sentences.

Read the text again and find meaningful endings.

a) After the Second World War, the Allies ____________________

____

b) The three western zones ____________________
and the Soviet zone ____________________

c) The people in the Federal Republic ____________________

____

d) The German Democratic Republic ____________________

e) The Berlin Wall was built because ____________________

____

f) If East Germans tried to escape to West Germany, ____________________

g) On the Monday demonstrations in 1989 ____________________

____

h) Because of a mistake made by a government spokesman on November 9, 1989 ____________________

____

i) Because it was a non-violent revolution ____________________

____

3. Find an expression in the text for ....

a) the most important city of a country: ____________________

b) a state whose politicians are elected by the people is a ____________________ state

c) the things that a person owns: ____________________

d) getting away from a place where you are not allowed to leave: ____________________

e) border: ____________________

f) putting somebody into jail: ____________________

g) a person who takes part in a public meeting to protest against something: ____________________

h) having enough money to buy things to make life comfortable: ____________________

i) at once: ____________________

j) passing from one side to the other: ____________________

4. Can you get it right?

In the following sentences there some mistakes. Underline them and correct them.

a) When people of the Federal Republic of Germany wanted to travel to Berlin, they could only travel by plane. ____________________ ____________________

b) West Berlin became the capital of the Federal Republic in 1945. ____________________

c) The East Germans could not buy a lot of things on the Internet or from catalogues. ____________________ ____________________

d) Millions of West Germans escaped from the GDR because of industrial problems. ____________________ ____________________

e) The inter-German border was one of the best guarded borders in Germany and controlled by soldiers on the Berlin Wall. ____________________ ____________________

f) East Germans were only allowed to travel to social countries. ____________________

g) Because of a mistake made by an East German government spokesman, thousands of East Germans crossed into West Berlin in 1990. ____________________

h) The East German government tried to stop the people from crossing into the west because it was a violent revolution. ____________________ ____________________

5. Explain in German.

One of your classmates is not very good at English. He has difficulties understanding the text. Help him and answer his questions in German.

a) ***Classmate:*** Ich habe das mit den Hauptstädten nicht ganz verstanden. Wie war das mit Berlin und Bonn?

You:

____

____

____

b) ***Classmate***: Was war denn genau der Unterschied zwischen dem Leben der Menschen in der BRD und der DDR?

You:

____

____

____

c) ***Classmate***: Warum hat die DDR die Mauer und die Grenzanlagen gebaut?

You:

____

____

____

d) ***Classmate***: Warum war die deutsch-deutsche Grenze eine der am besten bewachten weltweit?

You:

____

____

____

e) ***Classmate***: Was wollten die Montagsdemonstranten eigentlich erreichen?

You:

____

____

____

f) **Classmate**: Ich habe nicht verstanden, wie es dazu kam, dass sich die Grenzen am 9. November 1989 plötzlich öffneten.

You:

____

____

____

Lösungen

Henry, the happy snowman

Nr. 1

1m; 2h; 3l; 4n; 5j; 6a; 7o; 8i; 9b; 10g; 11d; 12c; 13f; 14k; 15e

Nr. 2

b) They fetched a carrot, some nuts, and two stones.
c) Suddenly the snowman began to talk.
d) She nearly started to cry because she was a bit frightened.
e) They didn't want to go home because they enjoyed the snow so much.
f) He crashed into Henry because he couldn't see where he was going.
g) Henry had a big hole in his belly.
h) They were sad because Henry was gone.
i) Mrs Taylor found a note from Henry.
j) Before the end of winter, he wanted to visit some more children.

Nr. 3

b) lunch = breakfast; hats = caps
c) cucumber = carrot; stones = nuts
d) street = garden
e) skateboards = sledges
f) bigger = smaller; belly = back
g) rain = snow
h) Tom = Ben; head = belly
i) Mrs Taylor = the children; back = belly; stones = snow
j) his parents = other children

Nr. 4

6f; 4g; 1b; 7h; 2a; 3c; 8e, 5d

The Royals

Nr. 1

1g; 2j; 3i; 4a; 5d; 6e; 7h; 8f; 9b; 10c

Nr. 3

				K	A	**T**	E				
					P	**H**	I	L	I	P	
						E	D	W	A	R	D
			G	E	O	**R**	G	E			
		V	I	C	T	**O**	R	I	A		
			L	A	D	**Y**	D	I	A	N	A
						A	N	N	E		
		C	A	M	I	**L**	L	A			
C	H	A	R	L	E	**S**					

The answer is The Royals.

Nr. 4

a) line 6/7: Elizabeth is not only the Queen of Great Britain but also of the 54 so-called Commonwealth countries.
b) line 13: After school he studied at Cambridge University.
c) line 18/19: Lady Diana was very popular and people called her their Queen of Hearts.
d) line 27–29: This was a holiday in the UK, so most people didn't go to work, and pupils didn't go to school.
e) line 26/27: They had been friends for a long time.
f) line 35–37: The majority of the British people are proud to have one of the oldest monarchies in the world, and most love their Queen.

Nr. 5

a) sovereign (monarch); b) Commonwealth countries; c) carriage; d) (helicopter) pilot; e) majority; f) wedding

A visit to Buckingham Palace

Nr. 1

1b; 2c; 3a; 4b; 5c; 6a; 7b; 8c; 9c

Nr. 3

1 'Her Majesty will soon be here to see you.'
2 'Please rise.'
3 'Be seated.'
4 'I am pleased to welcome you at Buckingham Palace today.'
5 'Here is a poster for every pupil.'
6 'I would like Steve Wilson to be the first.'
7 'I usually do not read so many letters personally.'
8 'I have got a special present for you.'
9 'Thank you, Ma'am.'

Nr. 4

a) Salisbury = Sittingbourne
b) book about her coronation = meeting
c) crown = Royal coat of arms
d) ten = five
e) working = on holiday
f) sat down = rose
g) alphabetical = chronological
h) nervous = excited
i) said hello to her = bowed
j) box = tea cup

Nr. 5

a) to borrow; b) (Your) Majesty; c) to enter; d) to bow; e) secretary

The bike trip

Nr. 1

a) wrong; b) right; c) right; d) wrong; e) right; f) wrong; g) right; h) wrong; i) wrong; j) wrong; k) right; l) right; m) right

Nr. 2

a) They wanted to go on a bike trip on their new mountain bikes. / to have a picnic in the forest.
d) They cycled nine miles before they turned into a forest path.
f) Nick's stomach hurt so much that he couldn't ride back home.
h) Before David could say anything, the mobile went dead.
i) He left it on for three days and forgot to recharge it.
j) Nick said, 'David, please don't leave me.'

Nr. 3

a) mobile; b) stomach; c) battery; d) picnic; e) tree; f) hospital; g) to cycle; h) far

Nr. 4

a) … decided to go on a bike trip (on their new mountain bikes).
b) … into his saddlebag.
c) … to the lake (first, perhaps swim in it and then have their picnic).
d) … drank some (of their) lemonade.
e) … the right side of his stomach.
f) … leaned against a tree.

g) … to cry.
h) … the mobile went dead.
i) … recharge it.
j) … find someone with a mobile. / … get help.
k) … don't leave me.'
l) … for almost two hours (but nobody came).
m) … Nick to hospital (where he had an operation the same day).

Nr. 5

1 Nick and David went on a bike trip on a Saturday morning.
2 Their mothers gave them something to eat and drink for a picnic.
3 Nick put his mobile phone into his saddlebag.
4 After nine miles on the roads, the boys turned into a forest path.
5 They wanted to go to a lake and have a picnic.
6 They drank some of their lemonade because it was hot.
7 Suddenly Nick felt a terrible pain in his stomach.
8 He couldn't go on because the pain was getting worse.
9 The battery of Nick's mobile was low.
10 When Mrs Carins answered the phone, Nick's mobile went dead.
11 David wanted to find help at the lake.
12 But Nick didn't want to stay alone.
13 Mrs Carins found the boys after more than two hours.
14 Quickly she took her son to hospital.

A photo of the monster

Nr. 1

a) wrong; b) wrong; c) right; d) right; e) wrong; f) right; g) right; h) wrong; i) right; j) wrong; k) right; l) wrong

Nr. 2

a) They arrived by bike.
b) They didn't go on a bike tour because it was raining.
e) Sam went into a café and David and Martin went into a souvenir shop.
h) He didn't see Nessie. He only saw a piece of wood.
j) Martin slipped into the water and his feet got wet.
l) They only turned their heads and looked at the boys.

Nr. 3

a) tourist; b) expensive; c) café; d) to shout; e) feet; f) wet

Nr. 4

a) … was bad;
b) … to the lake;
c) … it was too expensive for Sam;
d) … to a café;
e) … two plastic models of Nessie in a souvenir shop;
f) … to the lake;
g) … 'Look, the monster!' … a piece of wood;
h) … my plastic model in the water … a photo of it with his digital camera;
i) … the photo to Sam in the café;
j) … excited … all the other people at the café looked at us.

Nr. 5

3Ef; 4Aa; 8Be; 1Dh; 6Kc; 7Hg; 2Ib; 5Cd

King Henry VIII

Nr. 1

1f; 2i; 3j; 4g; 5e; 6d; 7h; 8a; 9b; 10c

Nr. 2

1 She was a Spanish princess.
2 She had a daughter who later became the first queen of England.
3 But nonetheless he married his second wife.
4 He made himself head of this new church.
5 She was accused of a love affair with her own brother and was executed.
6 But she died after she had given birth to a son.
7 Henry annulled their marriage after six months.
8 She had an affair with Henry's servant.
9 They married in 1543.
10 He was only nine years old.

Nr. 3

a) Henry Fitzroy; b) Catherine Howard; c) Catherine Parr; d) Anne of Cleves; e) Catherine of Aragon; f) Jane Seymour; g) (Lady) Elizabeth; h) Henry Fitzroy; i) King Henry VIII; j) (King) Edward; k) William the Conqueror; l) Anne Boleyn

Nr. 4

a) Because he needed an heir to the throne.
b) He broke with Rome and made himself the head of the Church of England.
c) Because she couldn't produce a male heir and only gave birth to a daughter.
d) Because she was accused of a love affair with her brother.
e) Because she was the love of his life and Henry was very sad after her death.
f) No, he wasn't. Henry had another son with one of his mistresses. His name was Henry Fitzroy.
g) He married her for political reasons.
h) Because she didn't protest against the annulment of her marriage to Henry.
i) Because the English parliament put them in the line of succession after Edward.

September 11, 2001

Nr. 1

a) wrong; b) right; c) not in the text; d) right; e) wrong; f) wrong; g) right; h) right; i) wrong; j) wrong; k) wrong; l) not in the text; m) right; n) wrong

Nr. 2

a) Two planes crashed into the Twin Towers of the WTC.
b) They were 411 m tall and had 110 floors each.
c) He usually sold them newspapers, cigarettes, hot drinks or sweets.
d) They thought that it was a terrible accident.
e) They couldn't get out because doors were blocked, walls had collapsed, some of the stairwells were destroyed and most of the lifts were not working anymore.
f) They died because the helicopters could not land there because of the smoke.
g) They jumped out of the windows and died.
h) The first tower collapsed at 09.59 and the second tower at 10.28 am.
i) He survived because he ran for his life when the first tower collapsed.
j) It didn't reach Washington because it crashed in Pennsylvania.

Nr. 3

a) earthquakes = catastrophes; b) café = newspaper shop; c) oldest = tallest; d) injured = dead; e) 09.20 = 09.02; f) policemen = firemen; g) fog = smoke; h) saw = didn't see; i) explosions = rubble; j) rubble = dust

Nr. 4

1 On September 11, 2001 Ron opened his newspaper shop at quarter to eight.
2 Not long after that two Boeing were kidnapped at Logan Airport in Boston.
3 At 08.48 am the first plane crashed into the north tower.
4 At that time about 17,400 people were in the buildings.
5 The people who saw the crash thought it was an accident.
6 The second plane crashed into the south tower at 09.02 am.
7 There were explosions and fires in both towers.
8 Firemen entered the buildings and tried to get to the upper floors.
9 But a lot of people couldn't get out of the buildings.
10 Others jumped out of the windows.
11 They all died.
12 At 09.59 the south tower collapsed.
13 Half an hour later the second tower collapsed.
14 People ran for their lives in order not to be killed by the rubble.
15 But most of Manhattan was covered in thick dust.
16 Because of the dust, Ron lost all his goods.

The sinking of the Titanic

Nr. 1

a) right; b) wrong; c) right; d) right; e) wrong; f) not in the text; g) right; h) wrong; i) not in the text; j) right; k) right; l) wrong; m) wrong; n) right; o) right; p) not in the text

Nr. 2

b) The Murphys left England because Mr Murphy had died in a coal-pit accident.
e) She woke up because she was thirsty.
h) They couldn't get back because many people were coming upstairs and blocking their way.
l) Patrick had disappeared.
m) She died when the ship sank.

Nr. 3

a) Because they wanted to start a new life with Mrs Murphy's sister in Philadelphia.
b) He had died in a coal-pit accident.
c) She paid for them with the insurance money from the mining company and the money they got for their furniture and their other belongings.
d) They stopped the third-class passengers from entering the upper class decks.
e) They heard a grinding sound and the ship trembled. / The Titanic hit an iceberg.
f) Because the people on the stairs blocked their way downstairs.
g) She learned that the Titanic had hit an iceberg and the ship was sinking.
h) She found strange that a band was playing a waltz while the other passengers were panicking on the promenade deck.
i) Because the girls were only wearing their night dresses.
j) There was a great noise and the stern began to rise out of the water. It slowly lifted high into the air and stayed there for about half a minute. Then many people jumped or fell from the ship.

Nr. 4

- Nora, Kate and Mrs Murphy shared a third-class cabin with the Skoog family.
- They wanted to start a new life with Nora's and Kate's aunt in Philadelphia.
- On April 14, 1912 at 11.35 pm Kate woke up because she was very thirsty.
- Nora and Kate wanted to find something to drink in their dining-room.
- Suddenly they heard a grinding sound and the Titanic trembled.
- The door to their dining-room was closed, so the girls wanted to go upstairs to a restaurant on B deck.
- After (they had gone up) two flights of stairs people came running upstairs from the lower decks because the lower decks were flooding.
- Kate and Nora could not warn their mother because more people came upstairs and blocked their way.
- A young man helped Kate and Nora upstairs to the promenade deck.
- The young man (also) found life vests for the girls and two seats in one of the life boats.
- Nora hoped that their mother was (would be) in another life boat.
- On April 15 at 02.20 am the Titanic sank.
- 1,503 people died, among them Nora's and Kate's mother.
- (The following morning) the (liner) Carpathia rescued 705 survivors and took them to New York.

Nr. 5

Musterlösung:

a) Because the third-class passengers should not mix with the rich first class passengers who had paid more for their trip and didn't want any contact with poorer people.
b) The Titanic was a modern ship and had a special construction.
c) The band helped to comfort the people on board with their music. Just before the ship sank it helped them to pray to God with the song 'Nearer my God to thee'.
d) Only women and children were allowed into the lifeboats. The rescue of the passengers was badly organized.

The big earthquake

Nr. 1

1 b, c; 2 a, c; 3 c; 4 a; 5 a, b; 6 b; 7 a, b, c; 8 a, b

Nr. 2

a) She didn't go to school because she had a sore throat, a runny nose, she hadn't slept much and didn't feel well.
b) Mr Sato was a manager in a computer shop and Mrs Sato was a shop assistant in a department store.
c) Because she had learned at school that in case of an earthquake it was important to seek shelter.
d) Because a shelf crashed next to her bed which made it more difficult for her to get out from under her bed, and she hoped that the ceiling would not come down on her bed.
e) Because there was no time. Mr Ito said, 'We must get out of here. It isn't over yet.'
f) She could see that a 20 foot wave had reached the quayside and crashed on the first houses, and that some cars that were coming behind them didn't make it because the water was so quick.
g) Because she lived north of Natori which couldn't be reached by the wave.
h) Because they were having a drink on the 5th floor of Mrs Sato's department store.
i) Because the night before the earthquake there was a report about earthquakes and tsunamis on TV.

Nr. 3

Textbeispiel:

- On March 11, 2011 Ayaka Sato didn't go to school because she didn't feel well.
- Her mother (Mrs Sato) prepared some food that she could eat when she was hungry.
- Then Mr and Mrs Sato went to work.
- Ayaka had something to eat and drink, watched TV and fell asleep after some time.
- She woke up because of a big earthquake and quickly crawled under her bed.
- A shelf crashed next to her bed so that it was difficult for her to get free.
- After the earthquake their neighbour Mr Ito helped Ayaka out from under her bed. Quickly they ran out of the house, and Mr Ito put her into his car.
- A big wave was coming from the seaside, but Mr Ito drove fast so that they escaped it.
- Ayaka called her parents. They had survived in a department store and were very worried.
- Two days later they picked her up at Mrs Ito's sister's.

Nr. 4

a) sore throat; b) outskirts; c) weak; d) neighbour; e) items; f) quayside; g) violent; h) (pieces of) furniture

Stop bullying me

Nr. 1

a) wrong; b) right; c) right; d) wrong; e) right; f) not in the text; g) wrong; h) right; i) right; j) wrong; k) right; l) wrong; m) not in the text; n) right; o) wrong; p) right

Nr. 2

a) She was very sad when she left.
d) She began to cry outside the cafeteria.
g) She didn't talk to her because she was frightened that the gang would bully her even more.
j) She stopped doing her homework so that the bullies couldn't tear it out of her exercise books.
l) She didn't want to steal the purse. She said, 'I'm no thief.'
o) She always had the feeling that Brenda meant mischief.

Nr. 3

a) nightmares; b) to pinch; c) bully; d) plain Jane; e) to punch; f) thief; g) satchel; h) classmate

Nr. 4

- They pinched her exercise books and tore out her homework.
- They dropped her food to the floor in the cafeteria.
- They called her names.
- They punched and kicked her.
- They took away her jacket on a rainy day.
- Brenda threatened her when she didn't want to steal her teacher's purse.

Nr. 5

- She didn't talk to her parents or her teacher.
- She asked the gang to stop bullying her.
- She stopped going to the cafeteria.
- She lost weight.
- She didn't do her homework.
- She had bad marks in her tests.

Nr. 6

a) Her parents didn't have much time. Her father worked hard and often came home late. Her mother was looking for a job and often wasn't at home when Valerie came back from school. They had their own problems and Valerie didn't want to worry them. Perhaps she feared that her parents would not understand her.
b) She didn't go to the cafeteria because the gang often bullied her there and threw her food to the floor. She didn't want to give them more chances to bully her there.
c) She was very unhappy and didn't feel good at school. She lost interest in her school work and in the tests because she could only think about the bullies. Perhaps she thought that if she didn't do her homework or learn for tests the gang would stop bullying her.

The Aboriginal people of Australia

Nr. 1

a) right, b) right; c) wrong; d) not in the text; e) wrong; f) not in the text; g) wrong; h) right; i) wrong; j) not in the text; k) not in the text; k) right; l) right; m) right; n) wrong; o) wrong

Nr. 2

c) They had no contact to the rest of the world. So they didn't trade goods.
e) When the Europeans arrived, between 300,000 to 1,000,000 Aboriginal people lived there.
g) They didn't understand the Aboriginal culture and wanted to teach them the British culture.
i) When the slaves were too old to work or became sick the British masters sent them away.
n) Their education still isn't as good as that of other Australians.
o) Twenty per cent of all prisoners in Australian prisons are Aboriginal people.

Nr. 3

a) … comes from the Latin word ab origine. / means the first or the earliest known. / describes the native people who have always lived there. / was first used in 1770 by the first Europeans who settled in Australia.
b) … had come from Indonesia during the ice age about 40,000 to 60,000 years ago.
c) … on the east coast of Australia because of the better climate.
d) … lived in smaller groups of 20 to 50 people.
e) … the invention of the returning boomerang and the didgeridoo.
f) … the European settlers arrived in Australia in 1770.
g) … wanted to teach them the British culture. / did terrible things to them. / took away their land.
h) … that the land the British took away from the Aboriginals didn't belong to anyone.
i) … were not allowed to vote in general elections. / mostly could not read or write.
j) … that Aboriginal children were taken away from their parents and put in foster homes where they were taught British culture and lifestyle.
k) … living in Australia today don't know anything about their true families.
l) … have their civil rights. / are allowed to live wherever they want to. / still belong to the poorest part of the Australian population. / still don't have a very good education. / have fewer chances to well-paid careers.

Nr. 4

a) Aborigine bedeutet der erste oder früheste Mensch, der in Australien bekannt war.
b) Die Aborigines kamen ursprünglich vermutlich während der Eiszeit aus Indonesien. Das liegt etwa 40 000 bis 60 000 Jahre zurück.
c) Sie lebten in Harmonie mit der Natur und hatten keinen Kontakt zu anderen Völkern. Sie lebten in Stämmen mit bis zu 700 Menschen, die sich wiederum in kleinere Gruppen mit bis zu 50 Menschen unterteilten. Sie waren Nomaden, Jäger, Fischer und Sammler.
d) Sie dachten, dass sie den Aborigines überlegen seien und bezeichneten sie als Wilde. Deshalb nahmen sie sich das Recht, sie zu versklaven.
e) Man wollte den Kindern die britische Kultur beibringen und das genetische Erbe der Aborigines „herauszüchten".
f) Die Aborigines sind immer noch schlechter gebildet als andere Australier und haben deshalb weniger Chancen auf gut bezahlte Berufe.

Nr. 5

- Line 1–6: Where does the name Aborigine come from?
- Line 7–20: Early Aboriginal life in Australia
- Line 21–34: The European settlers feel superior
- Line 35–41: The lost generation
- Line 42–49: Aboriginal life in the 20th and 21st century

German Reunification

Nr. 1

1b, c; 2c; 3a, c; 4b; 5a; 6a, b, c; 7b, c; 8a, b; 9c

Nr. 2

Musterlösung:

a) ... divided Germany and Berlin into four occupation zones.
b) ... became the Federal Republic of Germany ... became the Democratic Republic of Germany.
c) ... lived in wealth, built houses, bought cars and travelled to foreign countries.
d) ... was a socialist state and politically dependent upon the Soviet Union.
e) ... millions of East Germans had escaped to the Federal Republic during the 1950s.
f) ... they were shot on the spot.
g) ... Eastern Germans demanded better living and travel conditions.
h) ... thousands of East Germans went to the crossing points in East Berlin and crossed into West Berlin for the first time.
i) ... neither the East German government nor the Soviet Union tried to stop the people from reuniting.

Nr. 3

a) capital; b) democratic; c) property; d) to escape; e) frontier; f) to imprison; g) demonstrator; h) wealth; i) on the spot; j) to cross

Nr. 4

a) could only travel by plane = they could travel on transit roads
b) West Berlin = Bonn, 1945 = 1949
c) on the Internet = in shops; from catalogues = on the markets
d) West Germans = East Germans; industrial = economical
e) in Germany = in the world; the Berlin Wall = watch towers
f) social = socialist
g) 1990 = 1989
h) tried = didn't try; violent = non-violent

Nr. 5

Musterlösung:

a) Nach der Gründung der beiden deutschen Staaten 1949 wurde Ost-Berlin Hauptstadt der DDR und Bonn Hauptstadt der BRD. West-Berlin gehörte zur BRD.
b) Die Menschen in der BRD lebten im Wohlstand, weil die Wirtschaft wuchs. Sie bauten Häuser, kauften Autos und verreisten. Die DDR war ein sozialistischer Staat, der von der Sowjetunion abhängig war. Die Menschen hatten nicht viel Privateigentum und es gab nicht viel zu kaufen.
c) Die Mauer und die Grenzanlagen sollten verhindern, dass immer mehr DDR-Bürger in die BRD flüchten konnten.
d) Es gab Wachtürme und Grenzsoldaten. Flüchtlinge wurden oft sofort erschossen.
e) Die Montagsdemonstranten wollten bessere Lebens- und Reisebedingungen. Sie trugen Banner mit der Aufschrift „Wir sind das Volk".
f) Der Regierungssprecher sagte am Abend des 9. November, dass die Grenzen ab sofort geöffnet seien, anstatt erst ab dem Nachmittag des 10. November. Daher verlangen die Menschen die sofortige Öffnung der Grenzen, um nach West-Berlin zu kommen.